MUKEDI DIESTA - MPUTU Delphin

Computer networks:

MUKEDI DIESTA - MPUTU Delphin

Computer networks:

The world in our hands

ScienciaScripts

Contents

Since then, the scientific disciplines have always been at the heart of integral development in all areas and the lifeblood of every nation.

In turn, they give us the right to contribute to their expansion, which is fuelled or replenished by research, contacts, experience and acquired knowledge.

These days, information and communication technology (ICT), of which computers are a part, has a number of shortcomings, not least the lack of books, the backbone of most of our libraries and readers' houses, given that virtual libraries have not yet been set up, although not everyone will have access to them.

This information and communication technology is moving the whole world and all information systems to ensure that they are managed with peace of mind.

We have always been concerned to provide amateurs, professionals, learners and others with tools that can be used as guidelines, containing concise concepts or subjects.

This manual, which is accessible to all, contains at least the basic elements of computer networks, meeting the needs of those interested, including : materials/equipment,

data transmission, etc.

We will be proud to receive any comments or suggestions you may have, to ensure that continuity is the focus of every one of us, depending on the scientific circumstances.

"The Author

Introduction

Computer networks and telecommunications is one of the fields of business computing, and one that the whole world rejoices in.

As for the technicians in the profession, learners, researchers and others are experiencing enormous difficulties as a result of the lack of books in the field or in our libraries, as virtual books are not accessible everywhere.

So putting such a structure in the field is a way of overcoming these difficulties so that every user's operation will at least contribute something extra.

The computer and telecommunications networks that are shaking up all companies in terms of their performance and business, are helping and satisfying employers in the day-to-day life of their companies, something that was painful in previous years. To obtain a document, to consult a message, to follow a training course, to repair or buy an important tool, etc., it is necessary to travel long distances with all the possible risks.

Nowadays, everything is either in front of your nose or in the palm of your hand, thanks to this new technology, of which networks are an integral and seamless part.

The title: "***Computer networks: the world in our hands***" expresses this ease of being self-sufficient without going through the ordeals of the past. Now, all you have to do is connect to the networks, and at most there is a chance of finding the solution to the difficulty you are experiencing, even though the help of experts is so demanding.

We're putting our slightest computer knowledge on display, so that it can become a means of assistance, a work tool that can at least meet the needs of some and others.

This has been our great objective, gnawing at us all the time.

The aim of this book is to :

- demonstrate how computer networks came into being,
- give an idea of operating systems, even those used in networks ;
- explain the terms of networks, data transmission and their equipment ;
- and last but not least, wireless computer networks.

At the very least, it guides any operator to have a concrete image on the computer networks.

The question we often ask ourselves is what the country is doing for us. Frankly, without asking ourselves, this time we need to know what we are doing for the country.

In the words of Pierre Escoube: "after seriously considering the role of human capital in the country's process ... . . he believes that public administration is only as good as the people who make it up and whom they love[1] ". It's true that our companies have IT skills, and some of them are being trained to serve the world - let's encourage them.

All unfounded/unconstructive criticism ... when we have the appropriate skills to support the country in one way or another for its development. It's better to exploit what we have, so that we can make up for what's missing with the help of everyone.

---

[1] *Mukedi Diesta-Mputu Delphin, Conception d'un système informatique de gestion des impôts et taxes à payer d'une entreprise, Licence thesis, ISIPA, Kinshasa, 1994.*

1- Origin of the IT network

After two world wars: the first from 1914 to 1918 and the second from 1940 to 1945, international peace agreements were reached around 1946, averting a third war.

Despite this, cold war was brewing between the two major world powers: the capitalist bloc and the communist or socialist bloc, the United States (capitalists) and the Soviet Union, now Russia (socialists).

These two blocs, each with a group of countries at its back, were looking out for each other, so the United States, in order to protect its borders at all times (twenty-four hours a day), was looking for a system that could meet this crucial need. So they commissioned their army, above all, and anyone else they could find, to support them in this.

Man in general and scientists in particular remain the only masters authorised to deform nature, which after this deformation provides them with harmful consequences; in many cases, they experiment with their inventions, always using nature before the actual exploitation, i.e. before the application.

These scientists use animals, plants and insects for certain tests or experiments in research laboratories.

This was the case with Pasteur's smallpox vaccine[II] (.).

As for computer networks, the spider was targeted because of the way it spins its web, protects itself and feeds, and can fit into any corner.

So, any insect that bumps into the spider's web supplies itself with food, and if it is threatened, it escapes, or tries to depend on itself, in one way or another.

  Because it follows all kinds of movements of its web, whatever its size. location.

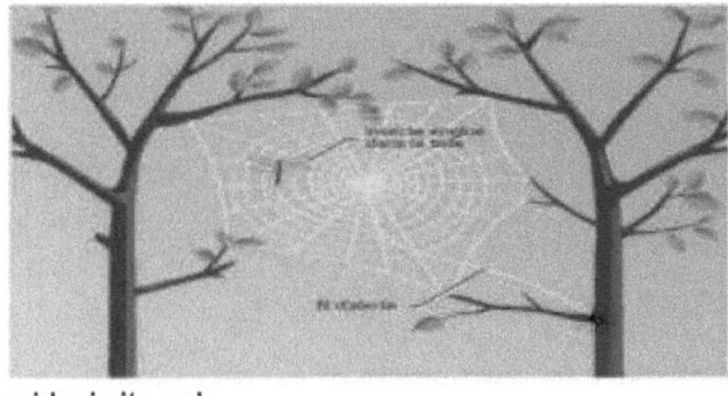

The spider in its web.

On the one hand, the American army[III] has always been structured and

---

[II] *Microbiology course, 4ᵉᵐᵉ Humanities*
[III] *Understanding the computer, What is the internet?*

flexible in terms of research, because we have to recognise that in the field of information technology, how many times has it contributed to the upheavals that have taken the whole world to the next level?

The observed wisdom is that the spider follows all the different movements of its web in all the different corners, and this transmission of information has prompted the American army to carry out research into computer networks.

On the other hand, the concept of the Web was developed by the European Centre for Nuclear Research (CERN) in 1991 by a team of researchers including Tim-Berners LEE, the creator of the concept of hyperlinks, now considered to be the founding father of the Web.

Tim Berners-Lee (Timothy Berners-Lee) is the co-inventor of the Web, which he developed in the early 1990s with his colleague Robert Cailliau, to enable their physicist colleagues at CERN (the European Laboratory for Particle Physics), where they were researchers, to exchange data and images rapidly, wherever they were in the world. In 1993, Tim Berners-Lee left this organisation and moved to the United States, where he taught at the University of California, Berkeley.
Computer and Communication Sciences at the Massachusetts Institute of Technology (MIT). He founded and directs the World Wide Web Consortium (W3C), an association of companies and individuals wishing to promote the use of the Internet.
promote the secure and democratic development of the Web.

Robert Cailliau, a Belgian computer engineer, is the   co-inventor of the World Wide Web (WWW), with its
British colleague Tim Berners-Lee. Developed in 1991 on the premises of CERN (the European Laboratory for Particle Physics) in Geneva, this interface enables users to navigate by clicking on   hypertext links.
(HTML language), the navigation system that underpins the Internet.

The "Web" is a contraction of "World Wide Web" (hence the acronym www) and is one of the possibilities offered by the Internet for browsing between documents linked by hypertext links.

The principle of the web is based on the use of hyperlinks to navigate between documents (called "web pages") using software called a browser. A web page is thus a simple text file written in a description language (called HTML), which allows the layout of the document to be described and graphic elements or links to other documents to be included using tags.

Thanks to Tim-Berners Lee's philosophy of the spider and the notion of the hyperlink, the research carried out led to the establishment of the structure of a computer and telecommunications network for the sharing of information and the exchange of hardware/peripherals.

2 - THE CONCEPT OF COMPUTER NETWORKS

A network is a set of interconnected objects. It allows elements to circulate between each of these objects according to well-defined rules.

• Network: set of computers and peripherals connected to each other (Note: two connected computers already constitute a network).

• Networking: Implementation of tools and tasks to link computers so that they can share resources.

Depending on the type of object, it is sometimes referred to as:

·   **transport network**: set of infrastructures and arrangements for transporting people and goods between several geographical areas

·   **telephone network**: infrastructure enabling voice to be transmitted between a number of telephones

·   **neural network**: a set of interconnected cells;

·   **criminal network**: a group of crooks who are in contact with each other (one crook usually hides another);

·   **computer network**: a set of computers linked together by physical lines and exchanging information in the form of digital data (binary values, i.e. coded in the form of signals that can take two values: 0 and 1). In computing, this is why we speak of a wired network and a wireless network.

CHAPTER I

OPERATING SYSTEMS

All operating systems have at least the same role and the same composition, a coherent set of programs that fulfil two main functions: to provide a set of services by presenting users with an interface adapted to their needs, and to carry out a certain number of preparatory operations to ensure exchanges between the various elements that make up a computer (the central processing unit, memory and input/output peripherals).

It manages the control of these devices by means of peripheral managers, more commonly known as drivers, which are integrated or added to it.

So any computer that does not have an operating system installed cannot meet the needs of the user. To do this, computer specialists call it "***First Basic Software***". To operate it on a network, a technical computer procedure must be applied, known as the network parameter/configuration.

1-The key roles of operating systems[IV]

In general, all operating systems have the same role, because they also have the same objectives:

- **Processor management**: the operating system is responsible for managing processor allocation between the various programs using a **scheduling algorithm**. The type of scheduler is totally dependent on the operating system, depending on the objective.
- **RAM management**: the operating system is responsible for managing the memory space allocated to each application and, where applicable, to each user. If there is insufficient physical memory, the operating system can create a memory area on the hard disk, called "**virtual memory**". Virtual memory makes it possible to run applications that require more memory than there is RAM available on the system. On the other hand, this memory is much slower.
- **I/O management**: the operating system unifies and controls program access to hardware resources via drivers (also known as peripheral drivers or I/O managers).
- **Application execution management**: the operating system is responsible for ensuring that applications run correctly, by allocating the resources they need to function properly. As such, it can "kill" an application that is no longer responding correctly.
- **Rights management**: the operating system is responsible for the security of program execution, ensuring that resources are only used by programs and users with the appropriate rights.
- **File management**: the operating system manages reading and writing to the file system and access rights to files by users and applications.

[IV] *Jean François P, CommentCaMarche, free computer encyclopedia, 2009*

- **Information management**: the operating system provides a number of indicators for diagnosing whether the machine is operating correctly.

2- Operating system components

The operating system is made up of a set of software programs that manage interaction with the hardware. This set of software generally includes the following elements:

- The kernel representing the functions

fundamental aspects of the operating system, such as memory management, processes, files, main I/O and communication functions.

- The command interpreter (Shell, as opposed to the kernel) enables communication with the operating system via a command language, so that the user can control peripherals while ignoring all the characteristics of the hardware it is using, the management of physical addresses, etc. or, for its part, gives instructions to the computer using commands to carry out a certain number of tasks while ignoring the technical characteristics of the hardware it is using. For example, it can be used to create, change, rename and delete directories on a disk, display a list of directories or examine their contents, etc.

- Traditionally, application programs were not an integral part of the operating system. But since the early 2000s, this view has changed among software publishers. The integration of Internet browsers, media players and firewalls in the latest consumer operating systems is a perfect example.

- The file system (FS), used to store files in a tree structure.

3- Different categories of operating system

An operating system is said to be "*multithreaded*" when several "**tasks**" (also called *processes*) can be run simultaneously.

Applications are made up of a sequence of instructions known as "*threads*". These threads are in turn active, waiting, suspended or destroyed, depending on the priority associated with them, or executed sequentially.

A system is said to be **preemptive** when it has a **scheduler** (also called a *planner*), which allocates machine time according to priority criteria to the various processes that request it.

The system is said to be **time-sharing** when a time quota is allocated to each process by the scheduler. This is particularly the case with multi-user systems, which allow several users to use different or similar applications simultaneously on the same machine: the system is then called a **"transactional system"**. To do this, the system allocates each user a time slot.

Multiprocessor systems

Multiprocessing is a technique that involves running several processors in parallel to obtain greater computing power than that obtained with a high-end processor, or to increase system availability (in the event of a processor failure).

SMP (*Symmetric Multiprocessing* or *Symmetric Multiprocessor*) is an architecture in which all the processors access a shared memory space.

A multi-processor system must therefore be able to manage memory sharing between several processors and also distribute the workload.

Embedded systems

Embedded systems are operating systems designed to run on small machines, such as PDAs (*personal digital assistants*) or autonomous electronic devices (space probes, robots, vehicle on-board computers, etc.), with limited autonomy. A key feature of embedded systems is their advanced energy management and ability to operate with limited resources.

The main "consumer" embedded systems for PDAs are : PalmOS; Windows CE / Windows Mobile / Window Smartphone

Real-time systems

Real **time systems**, mainly used in industry, are systems whose purpose is to operate in a time-constrained environment. A real time system must operate reliably within specific time constraints, i.e. it must be able to deliver correct processing of information received at well-defined time intervals (regular or irregular).

4- Types of operating system[V]

There are several types of operating system, depending on whether they are capable of simultaneously managing information of 16 bits, 32 bits, 64 bits or more.

System	Coding	Single-user	Multi-user	Single task	Multitasking
DOS	16 bits	X		X	
Windows3.1	16/32 bits	X			non-pre-emptive
Windows95/98/Me	32 bits	X			Cooperative
WindowsNT/2000	32 bits		X		Pre-emptive
WindowsXP	32/64 bits		X		Pre-emptive
Unix / Linux	32/64 bits		X		Pre-emptive
MAC/OS X	32 bits		X		Pre-emptive
VMS	32 bits		X		Pre-emptive

A network operating system is one that can access various network protocols, such as TCP/IP, IP "X, LanManagers, DecNet and so on. This sharing provides the same interests as those explained in the lines that follow, whereas this is what the computer network is all about.

[V] Mukedi Diesta-Mputu Delphin, Notes de Cours de Système d'exploitation Comparé, au deuxième Cycle Informatique (Réseau et Conception de Système d'Information) [unpublished].

CHAPTER 2

COMPUTER NETWORK CONCEPTS

There is no single type of network, because historically speaking there have been different types of computer, communicating in a variety of different languages, and also because the physical transmission media linking them can be very heterogeneous, whether in terms of data transfer (data traffic in the form of electrical impulses, light or electromagnetic waves) or the type of medium (copper lines, coaxial cable, fibre optics, etc.).

The benefits of a network

A computer is a machine for manipulating data. Man, a communicative being, quickly realised the advantages of linking these computers together to exchange information. This is one of the reasons why a network is useful:

A network makes it possible:

- File and application sharing ;
- Communication between people (via e-mail, live chat, etc.);
- Communication between processes (between industrial machines) ;
- Guaranteed uniqueness of information (databases) ;
- Multiplayer gaming, ...

Networks also make it possible to standardise applications, generally referred to as *groupware*. For example, electronic messaging and group calendars (Microsoft Schedule +) enable faster, more efficient communication. Here are the advantages of such systems;

- Reduce costs by sharing data and peripherals;
- Standardisation of applications ;
- Timely access to data,
- More effective communication and organisation;

Today, the trend is towards the development of wide area networks (WANs) deployed nationwide, or even worldwide. There are many advantages to this, whether you're a business or an individual...

The similarities between the different networks

The different types of network generally have the following points in common:

- **Servers**: computers that provide shared resources to users via a network server;
- **Clients**: computers that access shared resources provided by a network server ;
- **Connection medium**: determines the way in which the

computers are linked together;
- **Shared data**: files accessible on network servers ;
- **Printers and other shared peripherals**: files, printers or other items used by network users ;
- **Miscellaneous resources**: other resources provided by the server ;

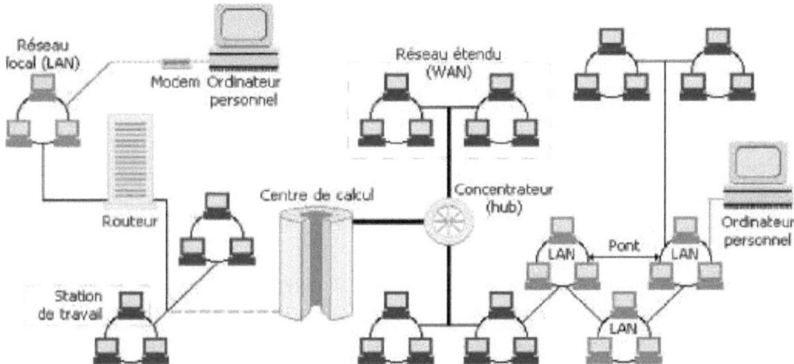

The topology of the Internet telematics network, based on the interconnection of a set of separate networks, makes it possible to interconnect an impressive number of computing machines throughout the world, which can exchange all kinds of information. Personal computers and workstations are connected to a Local Area Network (LAN), either via a dial-up connection using a modem and a standard telephone line, or via a direct cable connection to the LAN. There are other data transmission methods for connecting to a network, such as T1 lines or dedicated lines. Bridges and hubs link various networks together. Routers transmit data over networks and determine the best route to take it.

I - Topology

Let's understand something about this term: "Topology".
A computer network is made up of computers linked together by hardware: cables, network cards and other equipment to ensure the smooth flow of data. The physical arrangement of these elements is called the *physical topology, of* which there are three:

1. **Bus topology**
2. **Star topology**
3. **Ring topology**

A distinction is made between physical topology (the spatial, visible configuration of the network) and *logical topology.*
Logical topology represents the way in which data travels through cables. The most common logical topologies are Ethernet, Token Ring and FDDI.

1. **Bus topology**

A bus topology is the simplest way of organising a network. In a bus topology, all the computers are connected to the same transmission line via a cable, usually coaxial. The word "bus" refers to the physical line that connects the machines in the network.

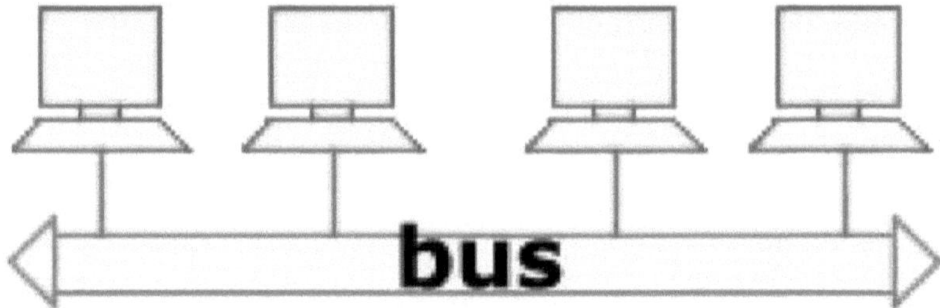

The advantages of this topology are that it is easy to implement and easy to operate, but it is extremely vulnerable because if one of the connections fails, the whole network is affected.

2. Star topology

In a star topology, the computers on the network are connected to a hardware system called a *hub*. This is a box containing a number of junctions to which cables from the computers can be connected. Its role is to ensure communication between the various junctions.

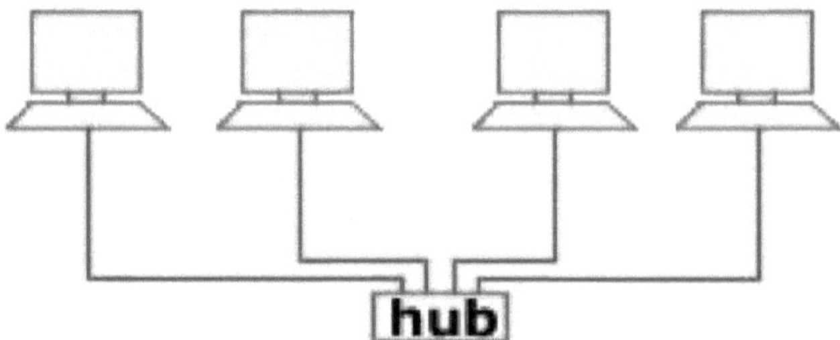

Unlike networks built on a bus topology, star topology networks are much less vulnerable because one of the connections can be easily removed by disconnecting it from the hub without paralysing the rest of the network. On the other hand, a star topology network is more expensive than a bus topology network because additional hardware is required (the hub).

3. Ring topology

In a ring topology network, the computers communicate one after the other, so we have a loop of computers on which each of them "speaks" in turn.

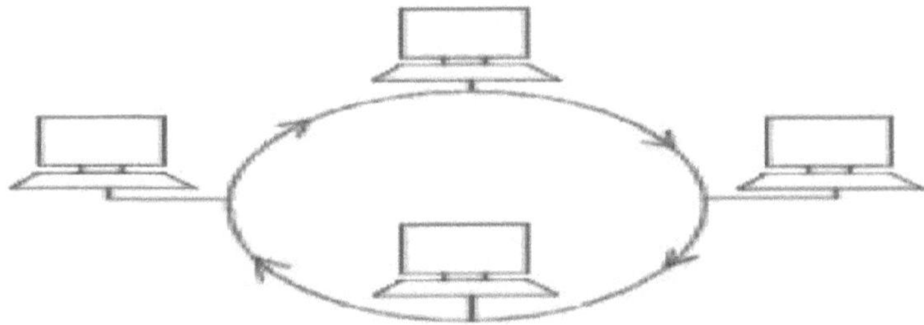

In reality, the computers in a ring topology network are not connected in a loop, but are connected to a splitter (called a MAU, *Multistation Access Unit*) which manages communication between the computers connected to it by allocating a talk time to each of them.

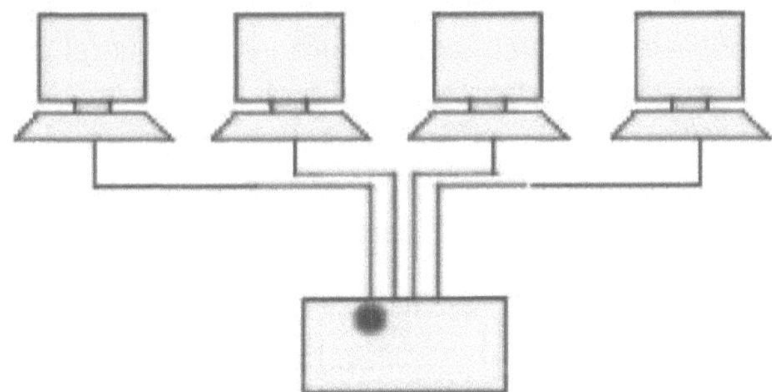

The two main logical topologies using this physical topology are Token Ring and FDDI.

2. Type of Network

There are different types of (private) network depending on their size (in terms of number of machines), data transfer speed and scope. Private networks are networks belonging to the same organisation. There are generally three categories of network:

. LAN (local area network)

. MAN (metropolitan area network)

. WAN (wide area network)

There are two other types of network: TANs (Tiny Area Networks), which are identical to LANs but less extensive (2 to 3 machines), and CANs (Campus Area Networks), which are identical to MANs (with maximum bandwidth between all the LANs in the network).

LAN stands for *Local Area Network*. This is a set of computers belonging to the same organisation and linked together in a small geographical area by a network, often using the same technology (the most common being Ethernet)...

A local network is therefore a network in its simplest form. Data transfer speed? of a local network can range from 10 Mbps (for an ethernet network, for example) to 1 Gbps (in FDDI or Gigabit Ethernet, for example). The size of a local network can be up to 100 or even 1000 users.

Extending the definition to the services provided by the local network, it is possible to distinguish between two modes of operation:

· in a *peer-to-peer* environment, where there is no central computer and each computer plays a similar role

· in a "client/server" environment, in which a central computer provides network services to users

LES MAN

MANs (*Metropolitan Area Networks*) interconnect several geographically close LANs (at most a few dozen km) at high speeds. A MAN allows two distant nodes to communicate as if they were part of the same local network.

A MAN is made up of switches or routers interconnected by high-speed links (usually fibre optic).

WANs

A **WAN** (Wide Area Network) interconnects several LANs across large geographical distances. The speeds available on a WAN are the result of a trade-off with the cost of the links (which increases with distance) and can be low.

WANs use routers to "choose" the most appropriate route to reach a network node. The best-known WAN is the Internet.

3 - Presentation of the architecture of a client/server system

Many applications operate in a client/server environment, which means that **client machines** (machines that are part of the network) contact a **server**, a machine that is generally very powerful in terms of input/output capabilities, which provides them with **services**. These services are programmes that provide data such as the time, files, a connection, etc.

Services are operated by programs, called **client programs**, running on client machines. The terms FTP client, email client, etc. are used to designate a programme running on a client machine, capable of processing information that it retrieves from the server (in the case of the FTP client, files, while in the case of the email client, electronic mail).

In a pure client/server environment, the computers on the network (the clients) can only see the server, which is one of the main advantages of this model.

Advantages of client/server architecture

The client/server model is particularly recommended for networks requiring a high level of reliability:

- **centralised resources**: because the server is at the centre of the network, it can manage resources common to all users, such as a centralised database, to avoid problems of redundancy and contradiction

. **better security**: because there are fewer entry points for accessing data

- **server-level administration**: as clients are of little importance in this model, they require less administration

- **a scalable network**: thanks to this architecture, customers can be removed or added without disrupting network operation and without major modifications

Disadvantages of the client/server model

Client/server architecture does have a few shortcomings, however:

- **high cost** due to the technical nature of the server

- **a weak link**: the server is the only weak link in the client/server network, given that the whole network is built around it! Fortunately, the server is highly fault-tolerant (thanks in particular to the RAID system).

How a client/server system works

A client/server system works as follows:

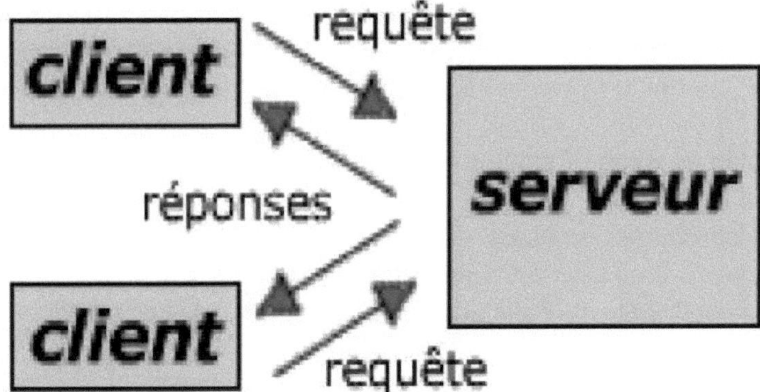

- The client sends a request to the server using its address and the port, which designates a particular service on the server.

- The server receives the request and responds using the address of the client machine and its port

Introduction to peer-to-peer architecture

In a *peer-to-peer* architecture, unlike a client/server network architecture, there is no dedicated server. So each computer in such a network is part server and part client. This means that each computer on the network is free to share its resources. A computer connected to a printer may be able to share it so that all the other computers can access it via the network.

Disadvantages of peer-to-peer networks

Peer-to-peer networks have a lot of disadvantages:

- the system is not centralised at all, which makes it very difficult to administer
- very little safety
- no link in the system is reliable

Peer-to-peer networks are therefore only suitable for a small number of computers (usually around ten), and for applications that do not require a high level of security (it is therefore not recommended for a professional network with sensitive data).

Advantages of peer-to-peer architecture

Peer-to-peer architecture does have a few advantages, however:

- low cost (the costs generated by such a network are equipment, cables and maintenance)
- foolproof simplicity!

Setting up a peer-to-peer network

Peer-to-peer networks do not require the same levels of performance and security as network software for dedicated servers. So you can use Windows NT Workstation, Windows for Workgroups or Windows 95, as all these operating systems incorporate all the features of a peer-to-peer network.

The implementation of such a network architecture is based on standard solutions:

. Placing computers on users' desktops

- Each user is their own administrator and plans their own security.

. This is generally a satisfactory solution for environments with the following characteristics :

. Less than 10 users

. All users are located in the same geographical area

. Safety is not a crucial issue

. Neither the company nor the network is likely to change significantly in the near future.

Administration of a peer-to-peer network

The peer-to-peer network meets the needs of a small business, but may prove inadequate in certain environments. Here are the questions to answer before choosing the type of network: The term "Administration" refers to :

1. User and security management
2. Provision of resources
3. Application and data maintenance
4. Installing and upgrading user software

In a typical peer-to-peer network, there is no administrator. Each user administers their own workstation. On the other hand, all users can share their resources as they wish (data in shared directories, printers, fax cards, etc.).

Safety concepts

The minimum security policy is to put a password on a resource. Users on a peer-to-peer network define their own security and, as all shares can exist on all computers, it is difficult to implement centralised control. This also poses a problem for overall network security, as some users do not secure their resources at all.

Two-tier architecture (also known as *2-tier architecture*, with *tier* meaning *third party*) characterises client/server systems in which the client requests a resource and the server provides it directly. This means that the server does not call on another application to provide the service.

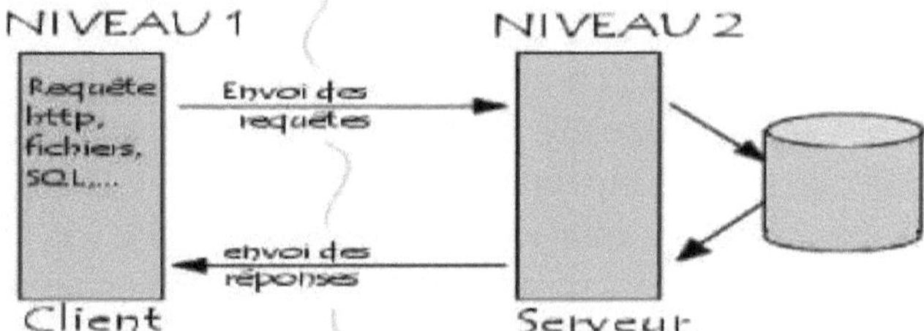

4. Presentation of the 3-tier architecture

In 3-tier architecture, there is an intermediate level, i.e. the architecture is generally shared between:

1. The customer: the demand for resources
2. The application server (also known as **middleware**): the server responsible for providing the resource but calling on another server.
3. The secondary server (usually a database server), providing a service to the first server.

NI VEAU 1   NI VEAU 2

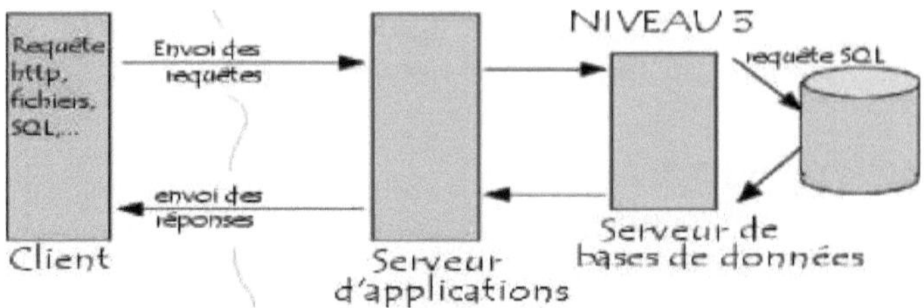

N.B.*: Given the widespread use of the term 3-level architecture, this can sometimes also refer to the following architectures:*

> Application sharing between client, intermediate server and enterprise server

> Application sharing between client, database intermediary, and company database

Comparison of the two types of architecture

The two-tier architecture is therefore a client/server in which the server is versatile, i.e. it is capable of directly supplying all the resources requested by the client. In the three-tier architecture, on the other hand, server-level applications are delocalised, meaning that each server is specialised in one task (web server/database server, for example). The three-tier architecture allows:

- greater flexibility
- greater security (security can be defined for each service)
- better performance (tasks are shared) **Multi-level architecture**

In 3-tier architecture, each server performs a specialised task (a service). This means that a server can use the services of one or more other servers to provide its own service. Therefore, the 3-tier architecture is potentially an N-tier architecture...

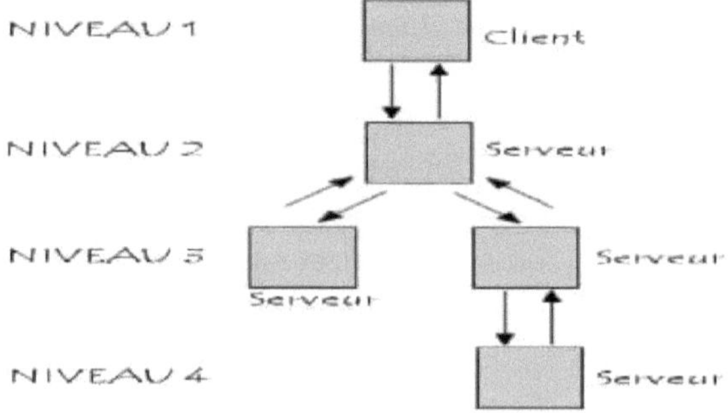

5- The virtual private network concept

Local area networks (LANs or LANs) are networks internal to an organisation, i.e. the links between machines belong to the organisation. These networks are increasingly linked to the Internet via interconnection equipment. Companies often need to communicate with geographically distant subsidiaries, customers or even staff via the Internet.

However, data transmitted over the Internet is much more vulnerable than when it travels over an organisation's internal network, because the path taken is not defined in advance, which means that the data travels over a public network infrastructure belonging to different operators. As a result, it is not impossible for the network to be eavesdropped on by an indiscreet user or even hijacked along the way. It is therefore inconceivable to transmit sensitive information for an organisation or company in such conditions.

The first solution to this need for secure communication is to connect remote networks using dedicated links. However, most companies cannot afford to link two remote local networks via a dedicated line, so it is sometimes necessary to use the Internet as a transmission medium.

A good compromise is to use the Internet as a transmission medium, using an "encapsulation" protocol (*tunneling*, hence the sometimes inappropriate use of the term "tunnelisation"), i.e. encapsulating the data to be transmitted in encrypted form. The network thus artificially created is referred to as a **virtual private** *network* (**VPN**).

This network is said to be *virtual* because it links two "physical" networks (local networks) via an unreliable link (the Internet), and *private* because only the computers on the local networks on either side of the VPN can "see" the data.

The *VPN* system therefore makes it possible to obtain a secure link at a lower cost, apart from the installation of terminal equipment. On the other hand, it does not provide a quality of service comparable to that of a leased line, since the physical network is public and therefore not guaranteed.

How a VPN works

A virtual private network is based on a protocol known as the *tunneling* **protocol**, i.e. a protocol enabling data passing from one end of the VPN to the other to be secured by cryptographic algorithms.

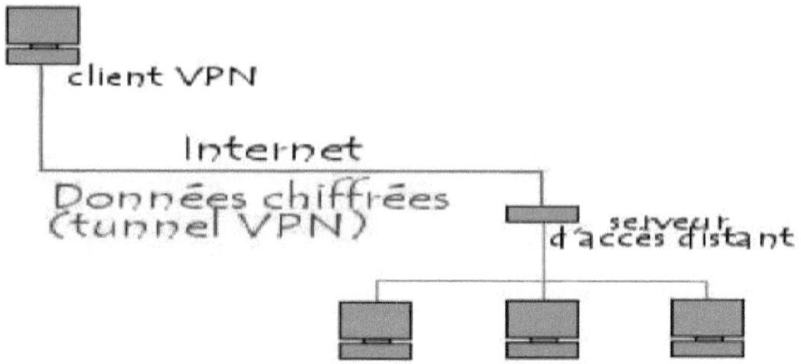

The term "tunnel" is used to symbolise the fact that between the entry and exit of the VPN the data is encrypted and therefore incomprehensible to anyone located between the two ends of the VPN, as if the data were passing through a tunnel. In the case of a *VPN* set up between two machines, the *VPN client* is the element that encrypts and decrypts the data on the user (client) side, and the *VPN server* (or, more generally, **the remote access server**) is the element that encrypts and decrypts the data on the organisation's side.

In this way, when a user requires access to the virtual private network, the request is transmitted in clear text to the gateway system, which connects to the remote network via a public network infrastructure and then transmits the request in encrypted form. The remote computer will then supply the data to the VPN server on its local network, which will transmit the response in encrypted form. On receipt on the user's VPN client, the data will be decrypted and then transmitted to the user.

Tunnelling protocols

The main tunneling protocols are :

. PPTP (*Point-to-Point Tunneling Protocol*) is a level 2 protocol developed by Microsoft, 3Com, Ascend, US Robotics and ECI Telematics.

. L2F (*Layer Two Forwarding*) is a level 2 protocol developed by Cisco, Northern Telecom and Shiva. It is now virtually obsolete

. L2TP (*Layer Two Tunneling Protocol*) is the result of work by the *IETF* (RFC 2661) to converge the functions of *PPTP* and *L2F*. It is therefore a level 2 protocol based on PPP.

. **IPSec** is a level 3 protocol developed by the IETF for transporting encrypted data over IP networks.

The PPTP protocol

The principle behind PPTP (*Point To Point Tunneling* Protocol) is to create PPP frames and encapsulate them in an IP datagram.

In this connection mode, the remote machines on the two local networks are connected by a point-to-point connection (including an encryption and authentication system), and the packet travels within an IP datagram.

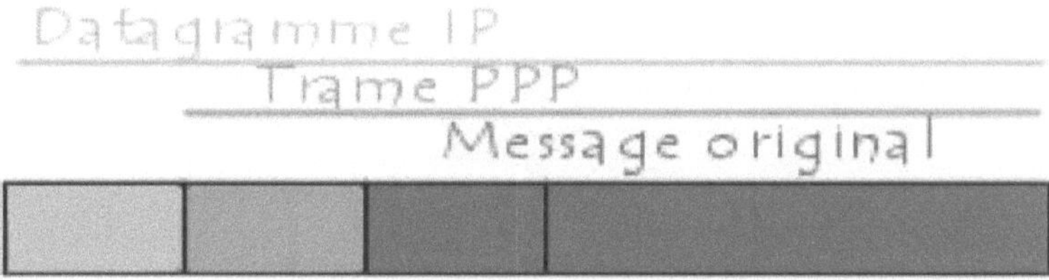

In this way, the local network data (as well as the machine addresses in the message header) are encapsulated in a PPP message, which in turn is encapsulated in an IP message.

The L2TP protocol is a standard tunneling protocol (standardised in an RFC) very similar to PPTP. The L2TP protocol encapsulates PPP protocol frames, which themselves encapsulate other protocols (such as IP, IPX or NetBIOS).

The IPSec protocol is a protocol defined by the IETF for securing exchanges at network layer level. It is a protocol that adds security enhancements to the IP protocol to guarantee the confidentiality, integrity and authentication of exchanges.

The IPSec protocol is based on three modules:

. *IP Authentication Header* (**AH**) concerning the integrity, authentication and replay protection of the packets to be encapsulated.

. *Encapsulating Security Payload* (**ESP**) defines packet encryption. ESP provides confidentiality, integrity, authentication and protection against replay.

- *Security Assocation* (**SA**) defining the exchange of keys and security parameters. The SAs bring together all the information on the treatment to be applied to IP packets (AH and/or ESP protocols, tunnel or transport mode, security algo used by the protocols, keys used, etc.). Keys are exchanged either manually or using the IKE exchange protocol (most of the time), which enables both parties to agree on the SAs.

5. The intranet paradigm

An intranet is a set of Internet services (e.g. a web server) internal to a local network, i.e. accessible only from workstations on a local network, or a set of well-defined networks, and invisible from the outside. It consists of using Internet client-server standards (using TCP/IP protocols), such as the use of Internet browsers (client based on HTTP protocols) and web servers (HTTP protocol), to create an information system internal to an organisation or company.

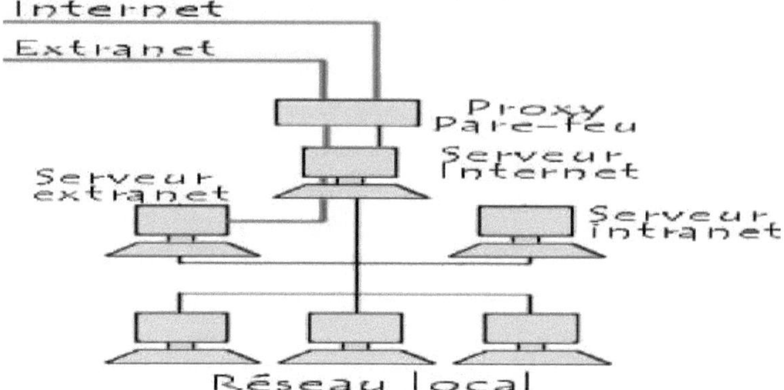

An intranet is generally based on a three-tier architecture:
- clients (usually web browsers)
- one or more application servers (middleware): a web server capable of interpreting CGI, PHP, ASP or other scripts, and translating them into SQL queries in order to interrogate a database
- a database server

In this way, the client machines manage the graphical interface, while the server handles the data. The network is used to transport requests and responses.

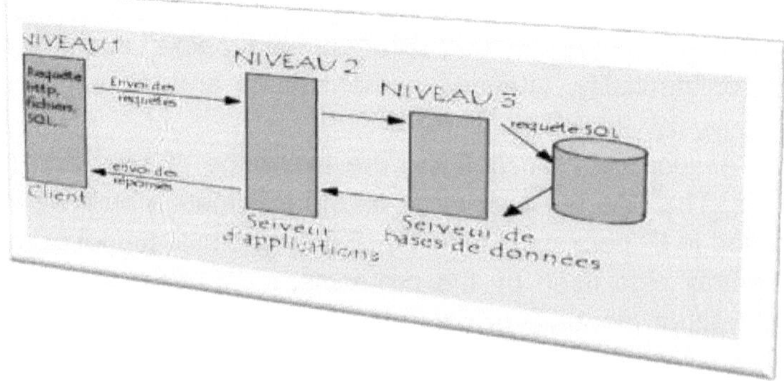

An intranet naturally has several clients (the computers on the local network) and can also be made up of several servers. For example, a large company might have a web server for each department, to provide an intranet consisting of a federating web server linking the different servers managed by each department.

The usefulness of an intranet

A company intranet makes it easy for employees to access a wide variety of documents, providing centralised and consistent access to the company's memory, in other words, *knowledge capitalisation*. In this way, it is generally necessary to define access rights for intranet users to the documents on the intranet, and consequently to authenticate them in order to give them personalised access to certain documents.

Documents of all types (text, images, video, sound, etc.) can be made available on an intranet. In addition, an intranet can perform a very interesting **"groupware"** function, i.e. enable collaborative working. Here are some of the functions that an intranet can perform:

- Provision of company information (notice board) ;
- Technical documents available;
- Documentation search engine ;
- Data exchange between employees;
- Staff directory ;
- Project management, decision support, diaries, computer-aided engineering ;
- Electronic mail ;
- Discussion forums, mailing lists, live chat ;
- Videoconferencing ;
- Internet portal.

In this way, an intranet promotes communication within the company and limits errors due to the poor circulation of information. The information available on the intranet must be kept up to date, avoiding version conflicts.

Benefits of an intranet

An intranet allows you to set up a low-cost information system (in concrete terms, the cost of an intranet can be reduced to the cost of the hardware, its maintenance and updating, with client workstations running free browsers, a server running under Linux with the *Apache* web server and the *MySQL* database server).

Secondly, given the 'universal' nature of the resources involved, any type of machine can be connected to the local network, and therefore to the intranet.

Setting up the intranet

An intranet must be designed according to the needs of the company or organisation (in terms of the services to be set up). In terms of hardware, all you need to do is set up a web server (for example, a machine running Linux with the *Apache* web server and *MySQL* database server, or Windows NT and the *Microsoft Internet Information Server* web server). You then just need to configure a domain name for your machine (e.g. intranet.your_company.com), install TCP/IP on all the client machines and define an IP address for them.

The extranet concept

An extranet is an extension of the company's information system to partners beyond the network.

Access to the extranet must be secure insofar as it provides access to the information system for people outside the company. This may involve either simple authentication (authentication by user name and password) or strong authentication (authentication using a certificate). It is advisable to use HTTPS for all web pages consulted from outside the company.

In this way, an extranet is neither an intranet nor an internet site. It is an additional system offering a company's customers, partners or subsidiaries, for example, privileged access to certain of the company's IT resources via a web interface.

CHAPTER 3

DATA TRANSMISSION

1- Introduction

Data representation

The purpose of a network is to transmit information from one computer to another. To do this, it is first necessary to decide on the type of coding for the data to be sent, i.e. its computer representation. This will differ according to the type of data, as it may be:

. Data source
- Textual data
- Graphic data
- Video data .

The representation of this data can be divided into two categories:

- A digital representation: i.e. the coding of information into a set of binary values, i.e. a sequence of 0s and 1s.
- Analogue representation: i.e. the data will be represented by the variation of a continuous physical quantity.

1- Data transmission medium

For data transmission to take place, there must be a transmission line, also known as a *transmission channel*, between the two machines.

These transmission paths are made up of several sections enabling data to be transmitted in the form of electromagnetic, electrical, light or even acoustic waves. The result is a vibratory phenomenon that propagates over the physical medium.

2- Transmission signal coding

For data to be exchanged, the transmission signals must be coded. This depends essentially on the physical medium used to transfer the data, as well as on the data integrity guarantee and the transmission speed.

3- Simultaneous data transmission

Data transmission is "simple" when only two machines are communicating, or when a single item of data is being sent. Otherwise, it is necessary to set up several transmission lines or to share the line between the various parties involved in the communication. This sharing is called multiplexing...

4- Communication protocols

A protocol is a common language used by all communication players to exchange data. However, its role does not stop there. A protocol also makes it possible:

.   Initiating communication
·   Data exchange
·   Error checking
·   A "courteous" end to communication

2- Physical transmission link

·   . What is a transmission channel?

A transmission line is a link between two machines. The term **"sender"** generally refers to the machine that sends the data and the term **"receiver"** to the machine that receives it. The machines can sometimes each in turn be receivers or senders (this is generally the case with computers linked by a network).

The transmission line, sometimes also called the *transmission channel* or *transmission path*, does not necessarily consist of a single physical transmission medium, which is why the end machines (as opposed to intermediate machines), known as *DTEs* (*Data Terminal Equipment*), each have equipment relating to the physical medium to which they are connected, known as *DCEs* (*Data Communication Equipment*). The set of *DCEs* on each machine and the data line is called a **data circuit**.

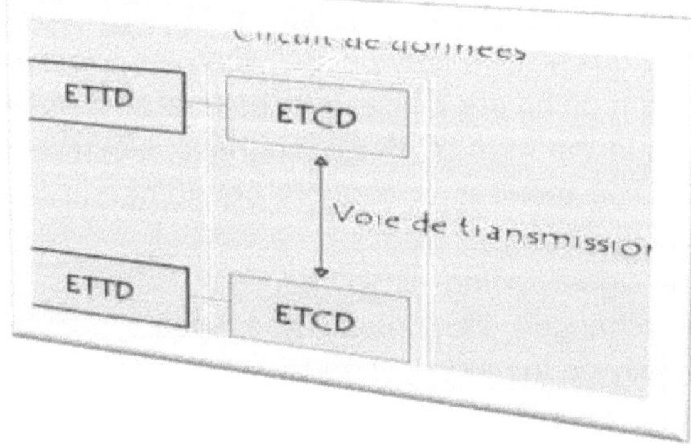

a- Basics of electromagnetic waves

Data is transmitted on a physical medium by the propagation of a vibratory phenomenon. The result is a wave signal that depends on the physical parameter being varied:

·   in the case of light, it is a light wave
·   in the case of sound, it is an acoustic wave
·   in the case of the voltage or intensity of an electric current, it is an electric wave.

Electromagnetic waves are characterised by their frequency, amplitude and phase.

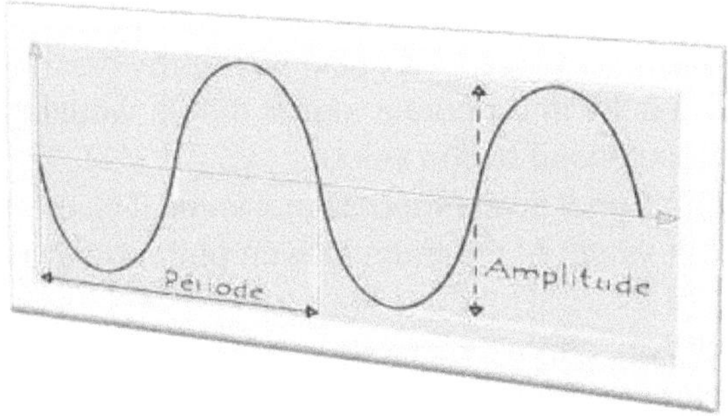

b- Types of physical media

Physical transmission media are the elements that enable information to be transmitted between transmission equipment. These media are generally classified into three categories, depending on the type of physical quantity they are used to transmit, and therefore on their physical make-up:

- **Wire supports** are used to circulate an electrical quantity on a cable, usually metal.
- **Aerial media** refer to air or vacuum, and allow the circulation of various electromagnetic or radio waves.
- **Optical media** are used to transmit information in the form of light.

Depending on the type of physical medium, the speed of propagation of a physical quantity will vary (for example, sound travels through air at a speed of around 300 m/s, whereas light travels at a speed of close to 300,000 km/s).

c- Disturbances

Data transmission over a line is not lossless. First of all, transmission time is not immediate, which means that data must be "synchronised" to some extent when it is received.

On the other hand, interference or signal degradation can occur.

- **Interference** (often referred to as *noise*) is any disturbance that locally alters the shape of the signal. There are generally three types of noise:

o **White noise** is a uniform disturbance of the signal, i.e. it adds a small amplitude to the signal whose average over the signal is zero. White noise is generally characterised by a ratio called the ***signal-to-noise ratio***, which expresses the percentage of amplitude of the signal in relation to the noise (its unit is the decibel). This ratio must be as high as possible.

o **Impulsive noises** are small peaks of intensity that cause transmission errors.

·   Signal **loss** represents the loss of signal energy dissipated in the line. The attenuation results in an output signal that is weaker than the input signal and is characterised by the value:

A = 20 log (Output signal level / Input signal level) The attenuation is proportional to the length of the transmission path and the signal frequency.

·   Signal **distortion** characterises the phase shift between the input signal and the output signal.

d- Bandwidth and capacity

The *bandwidth* of a transmission channel is the frequency interval over which the signal is not attenuated by more than a certain amount (generally 3 dB, because 3 decibels correspond to a 50% attenuation of the signal), so we have:

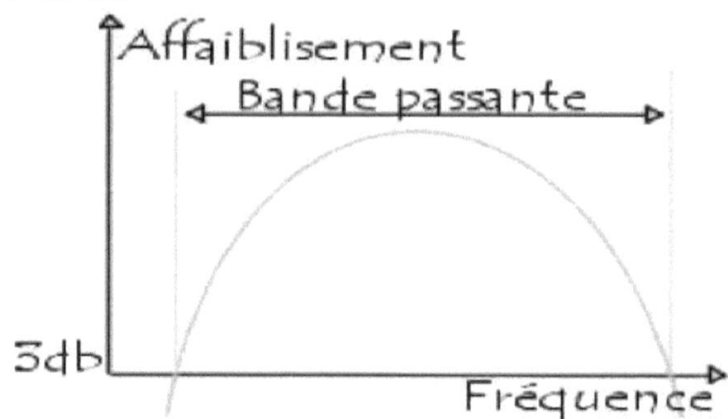

A telephone line, for example, has a bandwidth of between 300 and 3400 Hertz for a loss rate of 3 dB.

The capacity of a channel is the amount of information (in bits) that can be transmitted on the channel in 1 second. Capacity is characterised as follows: C= W log2 (1+ S/N)

·   C capacity (in bps)

. W bandwidth (in Hz)

·   S/N represents the signal-to-noise ratio of the channel.

e- Upload and download

Downloading is downward (from the server to your computer) and uploading is upward (from your computer to the server). It is interesting to note that uploading and downloading take place over separate transmission channels (whether over a modem or a dedicated line). So when you send a document (upload) you don't lose any bandwidth when downloading!

f- The principle of analogue transmission

Analogue data transmission involves transmitting information on a physical medium in the form of a wave. The data is transmitted via a *carrier wave*, a simple wave whose sole purpose is to transport the data by modifying one of its characteristics (amplitude, frequency or phase), which is why analogue transmission is generally called **carrier wave modulation transmission**. Depending on the parameter of the carrier wave that is varied, there are three types of analogue transmission:

. Transmission by carrier amplitude modulation

. Transmission by carrier frequency modulation

. Transmission by carrier phase modulation

Analogue data transmission

This type of transmission refers to a scheme in which the data to be transmitted is directly in analogue form. To transmit this signal, the DCE must continuously convolve the signal to be transmitted and the carrier wave, i.e. the wave it transmits is a combination of the carrier wave and the signal to be transmitted. In the case of transmission by amplitude modulation, for example, transmission is as follows:

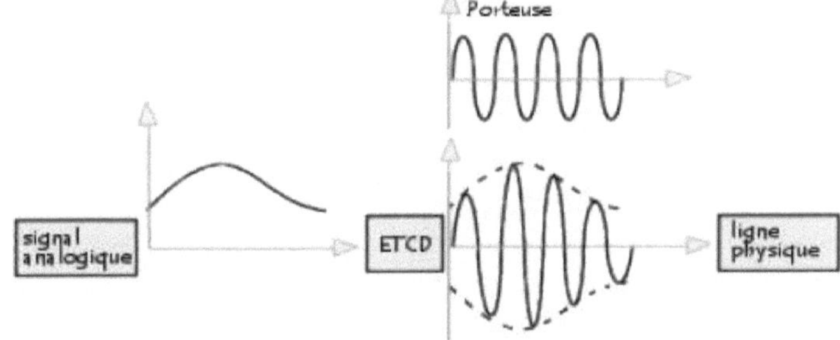

3- Analogue transmission of digital data

When digital data first appeared, transmission systems were still analogue, so a way had to be found to transmit digital data in an analogue way. The solution to this problem was the modem. Its role is:

. **On transmission**: to convert digital data (a set of 0s and 1s) into analogue signals (the continuous variation of a physical phenomenon). This process is called *modulation*.

. **On reception**: to convert the analogue signal into digital data. This process is called *demodulation*.

1- Introduction to digital transmission

Digital transmission involves transmitting information on the physical communication medium in the form of digital signals. Analogue data

must first be digitised before it can be transmitted. However, digital information cannot be transmitted in the form of 0s and 1s directly, so it has to be encoded in the form of a signal with two states, for example:
- two voltage levels with respect to earth
- the voltage difference between two wires
- the presence/absence of current in a wire
- the presence/absence of light . . .

This transformation of binary information into a two-state signal is carried out by the DCE, also known as the *baseband encoder*, hence the term *baseband transmission* for digital transmission...

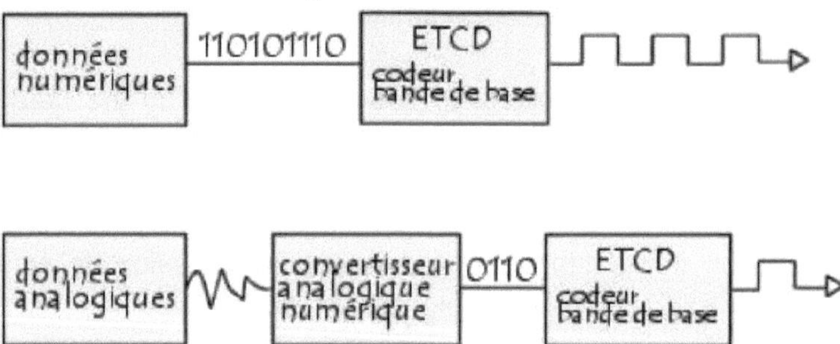

Signal coding

For transmission to be optimal, the signal must be coded in such a way as to facilitate its transmission on the physical medium. There are various coding systems for this purpose, which can be divided into two categories:

- Two-level coding: the signal can only take on a strictly negative or strictly positive value (-X or +X, where X represents a value of the physical quantity used to transport the signal).
- Three-level coding: the signal can take on a value of

strictly negative, zero or strictly positive (-X, 0 or +X)

NRZ coding

NRZ coding (which stands for *No Return to Zero*) is the first and simplest coding system. It simply transforms 0s into -Xs and 1s into +Xs, giving a bipolar coding system in which the signal is never zero. As a result, the receiver can determine whether or not a signal is present.

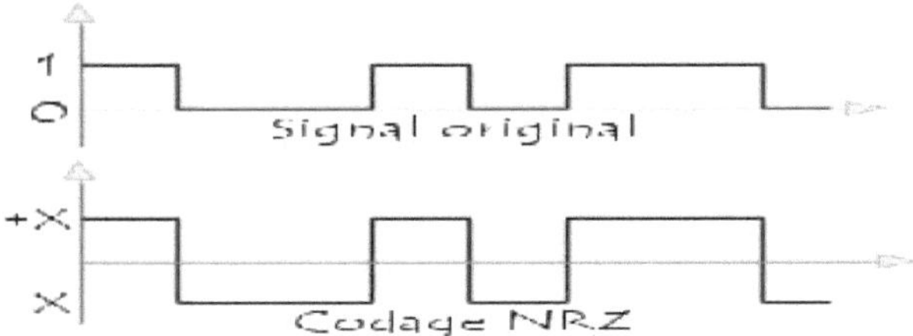

NRZI coding

NRZI coding is significantly different from NRZ coding. With this encoding, when the bit is set to 1, the signal changes state after the clock has topped. When the bit is 0, the signal undergoes no change of state.

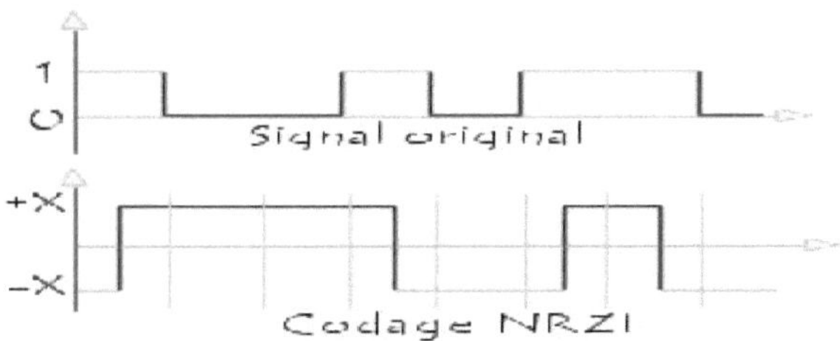

NRZI coding has a number of advantages, including
- Detecting the presence or absence of the signal
- The need for a low signal transmission current

However, it does have one drawback: the presence of a DC current during a sequence of zeros, which interferes with synchronisation between transmitter and receiver.

Manchester coding

Manchester coding, also known as *biphase coding* or *PE* (for *Phase Encode*), introduces a transition in the middle of each interval. It involves an exclusive OR (XOR) between the signal and the clock signal, resulting in a rising edge when the bit is zero, and a falling edge otherwise.

Manchester coding has a number of advantages, including
- non-zero crossing, enabling the receiver to detect a signal

- a wide-band spectrum

Delay Mode coding (de Miller)

Delay Mode coding, also known as *Miller coding*, is similar to Manchester coding, except that a transition appears in the middle of the interval only when the bit is set to 1. This allows higher data rates...

Simple bipolar coding

Simple bipolar coding is a three-level coding. It therefore offers three states of the quantity transported on the physical medium:

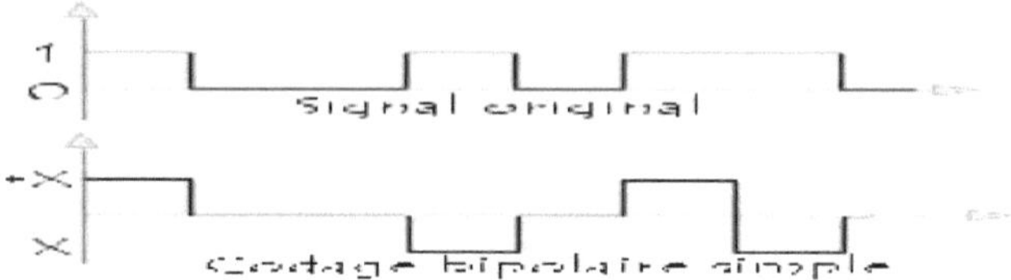

- The value *0* when the bit is set to 0
- Alternatively X and -X when the bit is 1

4- Wiring

1- The different types of cabling

To link the various entities in a network, several physical data transmission media can be used. One of these is the use of cables. There are many different types of cable, but a general distinction is made between them:

- Coaxial cable
- Ladouble twisted pair
- Optical fibre

2- Coaxial cable

Coaxial *cable* has long been the cabling of choice, for the simple reason that it is inexpensive and easy to handle (weight, flexibility, etc.).

A coaxial cable consists of a central part (called the *core*), i.e. a copper wire wrapped in insulation, then a braided metal shield and finally an outer sheath.

- **The sheath** protects the cable from the outside environment. It is usually made of rubber (sometimes polyvinyl chloride (PVC), and sometimes Teflon).
- **The shielding** (metal sheathing) around the cables protects the data transmitted over the medium from interference (otherwise known as *noise*) that can cause data distortion.
- **The insulator** surrounding the central part is made of a dielectric material to prevent any contact with the shielding, causing electrical interactions (short-circuit).
- **The core**, which carries the data, is generally made up of a single copper strand or several twisted strands.

Thanks to its shielding, coaxial cable can be used over long distances and at high speeds (unlike twisted-pair cable), although it is reserved for basic installations.

It should be noted that there are coaxial cables with double shielding (one insulating layer, one shielding layer) and coaxial cables with quadruple shielding (two insulating layers, two shielding layers). There are usually two types of coaxial cable:

- The **10Base2 - thin coaxial cable** (called *Thinnet*, or *CheaperNet*) is a thin diameter cable (6 mm), conventionally white (or greyish) in colour. It is highly flexible and can be used in most networks by connecting it directly to the network card. It can carry a signal over a distance of around 185 metres without attenuation.

It is part of the RG-58 family, with an impedance (resistance) of 50 ohms. The different types of fine coaxial cable are distinguished according to the central part of the cable (core).

Cable	Description
RG-58 / U	Central strand made up of a single copper strand
RG-58 A/U	Twisted
RG-58 C/U	Military version of the RG-58 A/U
RG-59	Broadband transmission (cable TV)

RG-6	Wider diameter, recommended for higher frequencies than RG-59
RG-62	Arcnet network

. The **10Base5 - thick coaxial cable** (*Thicknet* or

Thick Ethernet (also known as *Yellow Cable*, because of its conventional yellow colour) is a shielded cable with a larger diameter (12 mm) and an impedance of 50 ohms. It has long been used in Ethernet networks, earning it the name "Standard Ethernet Cable". Because its core has a larger diameter, the distance likely to be covered by the signals is greater, enabling it to transmit signals over a distance of up to 500 metres without attenuation (without signal re-amplification). It has a bandwidth of 10 Mbps and is therefore often used as a backbone cable to link small networks of computers connected via Thinnet. However, given its diameter, it is less flexible than Thinnet.

Transceiver: the connection between Thinnet and Thicknet

The connection between Thinnet and Thicknet is made using a **transceiver**. This is fitted with a so-called "*vampire*" plug which makes the actual physical connection to the central part of the Thinnet by piercing the insulating casing. The transceiver cable (*drop cable*) is connected to an **AUI** (*Attachment Unit Interface*) connector, also known as a **DIX** (Digital Intel Xerox) or **DB 15** (*SUB-D 15*) connector.

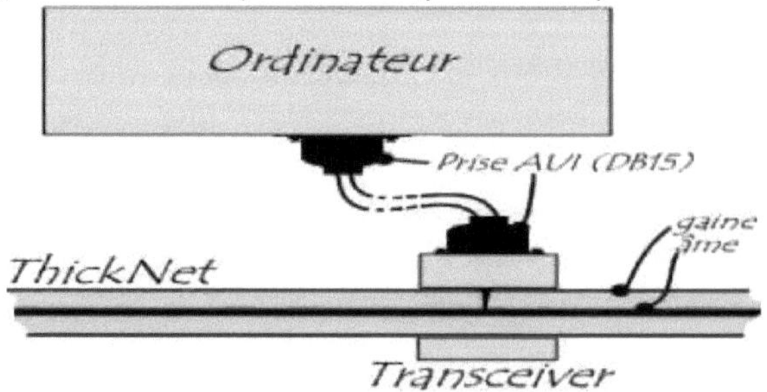

Connectors for coaxial cable

Thinnet and Thicknet both use **BNC** connectors (*Bayonet-Neill-Concelman* or *British Naval Connector*) to link cables to computers.

The BNC family includes :

.BNC cable connector: soldered or crimped to the end of the cable.

• BNC T connector: connects the computer network card to the network cable.

• BNC extender: connects two segments of coaxial cable to form a longer cable.

• BNC termination plug: placed at each end of a bus network cable to absorb unwanted signals. It is connected to earth. A bus network cannot operate without it. It would be put out of service.

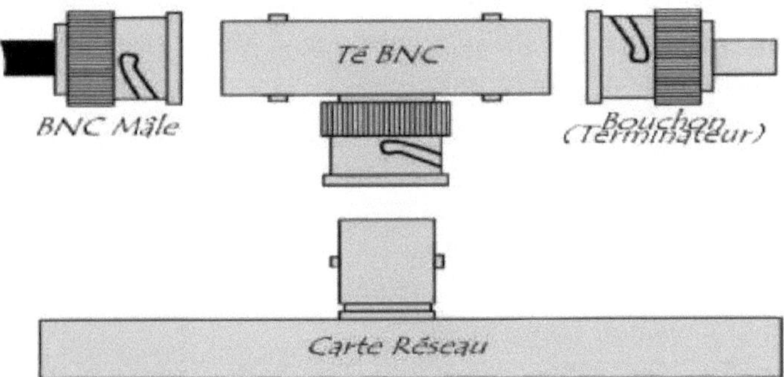

Twisted pair cabling

In its simplest form, *twisted-pair* cable consists of two strands of copper twisted together and covered with insulation.

There are generally two types of twisted pair:

- Shielded Twisted-Pair (**STP**) ;
- Unshielded Twisted-Pair (**UTP**).

A cable is often made from several twisted pairs grouped together and placed inside the protective sheath.

Interleaving eliminates noise (electrical interference) from adjacent pairs or other sources (motors, relays, transformers).

The twisted pair is therefore suitable for setting up a local network for a small number of users with a limited budget and simple connectors. However, over long distances and at high data rates, it cannot guarantee data integrity (i.e. transmission without data loss).

Unshielded twisted pair (UTP)

UTP cable complies with the 10BaseT specification. It is the most widely used type of twisted pair for local area networks. Here are a few characteristics:

- Maximum segment length: 100 metres
- Composition: 2 insulated copper wires
- UTP standards: determine the number of twists per foot (33 cm) of cable depending on the intended use.
- UTP: listed in EIA/TIA (Electronic Industries Association / Telecommunications Industries Association) Commercial Building Wiring Standard 568. The EIA/TIA 568 standard has used UTP to create standards applicable to all kinds of premises and cabling contexts,

providing the public with a guarantee of product consistency. These standards include five categories of UTP cable:

- **Category 1**: Traditional telephone cable (voice transfer but no data)
- **Category 2**: Data transmission at up to 4 Mbit/s (ISDN). This type of cable is made up of 4 twisted pairs.
- **Category3** : 10Mbit/smaximum . Thiscabletypeis consisting of 4 twisted pairs and 3 twists per leg
- **Category4** : 16Mbit/smaximum . Thiscabletypeis consisting of 4 twisted copper pairs
- **Category5** : 100Mbit/smaximum . Thiscabletypeis consisting of 4 twisted copper pairs

- **Category 5e**: 1000 Mbit/s maximum. This type of cable is made up of 4 twisted copper pairs. Most telephone installations use UTP cable.

Many premises are pre-wired for this type of installation

(often in sufficient numbers to meet future needs). If the pre-installed twisted pair is of good quality, it is possible to transfer data and therefore use it in a computer network. However, attention must be paid to the number of twists and other electrical characteristics required for quality data transmission. The main problem is that UTP cable is particularly prone to interference (signals from one line mixing with those from another). The only solution is shielding. Shielded twisted pair (STP)

STP (*Shielded Twisted Pair*) cable uses a better quality, more protective copper sheath than the sheath used by UTP cable. It contains a protective sheath between and around the pairs. In STP cable, the copper wires of a pair are themselves twisted, which provides STP cable with excellent shielding,   i.e. better protection against electromagnetic interference.

interference). It also enables faster transmission over longer distances. Twisted pair connectors

The twisted pair is connected using an RJ-45 connector. This connector is similar to the RJ-11 used in telephony, but different in certain respects: the RJ-45 is slightly larger and cannot be inserted into an RJ-11 telephone socket. What's more, the RJ-45 has eight pins, whereas the RJ-11 generally has only six or even four.

3- Fibre optics

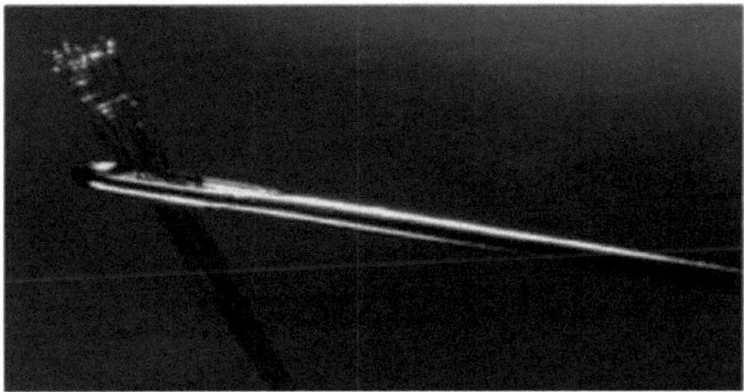

From the 1950s onwards, optical fibres were widely used in scientific, medical and industrial research. These high refractive index glass fibres, placed parallel to each other and separated by thin layers of low refractive index glass, can transmit electromagnetic signals (including light) with almost no loss and at very high speeds. Endoscopes are equipped with such fibres, making it easier to examine cavities in the human body that are normally inaccessible. Optical fibres are now used in telecommunications, and have a great future ahead of them. Combined with lasers, for example, they are used in long-distance telephony and remote computing.   :

- Lightweight
- Noise immunity
- Low attenuation
- Tolerates data rates of around 100 Mbps
- Bandwidth from a few tens of megahertz to several gigahertz (single-mode fibre)

Optical cabling is particularly well-suited to links between distribution centres (the central link between several buildings, known as the *backbone*) because it allows connections over long distances (from a few kilometres to 60 km in the case of single-mode fibre) without the need for earthing. What's more, this type of cable is very secure, as it is extremely difficult to tap into.

However, despite its mechanical flexibility, this type of cable is not suitable for connections in a local area network because it is difficult to install and expensive. This is why twisted pair or coaxial cable is preferred for small links.

5 - Multiplexing

Multiplexing refers to the ability to transmit data from several pairs of equipment (transmitters and receivers) on a single physical medium (called a *high-speed channel*); these are then referred to as *low-speed channels*.

A *multiplexer* is the multiplexing equipment used to combine the signals from the transmitters for transmission on the *high-speed channel*. The multiplexing equipment on which the receivers are connected to the *high-speed channel* is called a *demultiplexer*.

Frequency multiplexing

Frequency *Division Multiplexing* (*FDM*), also known as *MRF*, allows the frequency band available on the high-speed channel to be divided into a series of narrower channels, so that signals from the various low-speed channels can be continuously transmitted on the high-speed channel.

This process is used in particular on telephone lines and physical twisted-pair links to increase throughput. Time-division multiplexing

Time-division multiplexing (*TDM*) allows signals from different low-speed channels to be sampled and transmitted successively on the high-speed channel, allocating the entire bandwidth to them, even if they have no data to transmit.

Statistical multiplexing

Statistical multiplexing has the same characteristics as time-division multiplexing, except that only those low-speed channels containing data are transmitted on the high-speed channel. The name of this type of multiplexing comes from the fact that the multiplexers are based on statistics about the throughput of each low-speed line. As the high-speed line does not transmit the *blanks*, performance is better than with time-division multiplexing.

CHAPTER 4

COMPUTER NETWORK EQUIPMENT

1- Presentation

A local **area network** (*LAN*) is a network used to interconnect computers within a company or organisation. Thanks to this concept, which dates back to 1970, the employees of a company have at their disposal a system that allows..:

- Exchange information
- To communicate
- Access to a range of services

A local area network generally connects computers (or resources such as printers) using wired transmission media (twisted pair or coaxial cables in most cases) over a circumference of around a hundred metres. Beyond that, the network is considered to be part of another category of network known as a MAN (*metropolitan area network*), for which the transmission media are better suited to long distances...

2- The hardware components of a local network

A local area network is made up of computers linked by a set of hardware and software components. The hardware elements used to interconnect computers are as follows:

- **The network card** (sometimes called a *coupler*): this is a card connected to the computer's motherboard, enabling it to interface with the physical medium, i.e. the physical lines used to transmit the information.
- **The transceiver** (also known as **an** *adapter*): this transforms the signals travelling on the physical medium into logical signals that can be manipulated by the network card, both on transmission and reception:
- **The socket**: this is the element that provides the mechanical link between the network card and the physical medium.
- **The physical interconnection medium**: this is the medium (usually wired, i.e. in the form of a cable) used to link computers together   .

The main physical media

used in local networks are as follows:

- o The   coaxial cable
- o Twisted Shield
- o Optical fibre

3- Local network topologies

Hardware devices alone are not enough to use a local network. It is necessary to define a standard method of access between the

computers, so that they know how the computers exchange information, particularly when more than two computers share the physical medium. This access method is called **logical topology**. Logical topology is achieved by an **access protocol**. The most commonly used access protocols are:
- Ethernet
- Token ring

The way in which computers are physically interconnected is called their **physical topology**. The basic physical topologies are:
- Ring topology
- Bus topology
- Star topology

4- Network Interconnection

1- Interconnection

The need for interconnection

A local network is used to interconnect an organisation's computers. However, an organisation generally has several local networks, so it is sometimes essential to link them together. In this case, specific equipment is required.

In the case of two networks of the same type, it is sufficient to pass the frames from one to the other. In the opposite case, i.e. when the two networks use different protocols, it is essential to carry out a protocol conversion before transferring the frames. The equipment to be used will therefore vary depending on the configuration. Interconnection equipment

The main hardware devices used in local networks are:
- Repeaters, for regenerating a signal
- Hubs, for connecting several hosts together
- Bridges, used to link local networks of the same type
- Switches to connect various elements while segmenting the network
- Gateways, used to link local networks of different types
- Routers, to link up a number of local networks in such a way as to allow data to flow from one network to another in the best possible way
- B-router, combining the functions of a router and a bridge

2- Repeaters

On a transmission line, the greater the distance between two active elements, the greater the distortion and attenuation of the signal. Generally, two nodes in a local network cannot be more than a few hundred metres apart, which is why additional equipment is required beyond this distance.

A *repeater* is a simple piece of equipment used to regenerate a signal between two network nodes, in order to extend the cabling distance of a network. The repeater only works at the physical level (layer 1 of the OSI model), i.e. it only works at the level of the binary information circulating on the transmission line and is not capable of interpreting the packets of information.

On the other hand, a repeater can be used to form an interface between two different types of physical media, i.e. it can, for example, be used to connect a twisted pair segment to a fibre optic strand.

3- The **concentrator**

A **concentrator** is a piece of hardware that concentrates network traffic from several hosts and regenerates the signal. The concentrator is an entity with a certain number of ports (it has as many ports as it can connect machines together, generally 4, 8, 16 or 32). Its sole purpose is to recover the binary data arriving on a port and distribute it to all the ports. Like the repeater, the concentrator operates at level 1 of the OSI model, which is why it is sometimes called a *multi-port repeater*.

The concentrator is used to connect several machines together, sometimes in a star configuration, which is why it is called a *hub*, to illustrate the fact that it is the point where communications between the different machines pass through.

1- Type of concentrators

There are several categories of concentrators:

- **Active**" concentrators: these are powered by electricity and regenerate the signal on the various ports.
- So-called **"passive"** concentrators   : they can only be used to broadcast the signal to all connected hosts without amplification

2- Connecting several hubs

It is possible to connect several hubs together in order to concentrate a larger number of machines, known as *daisy* chains. To do this, simply connect the hubs using a crossover cable, i.e. a cable linking the receive connectors at one end to the receive connectors at the other.

Hubs are generally equipped with a special port called *"uplink"*, enabling a straight cable to be used to connect two hubs together. There are also hubs that automatically cross or uncross their ports depending on whether they are connected to a host or a hub.

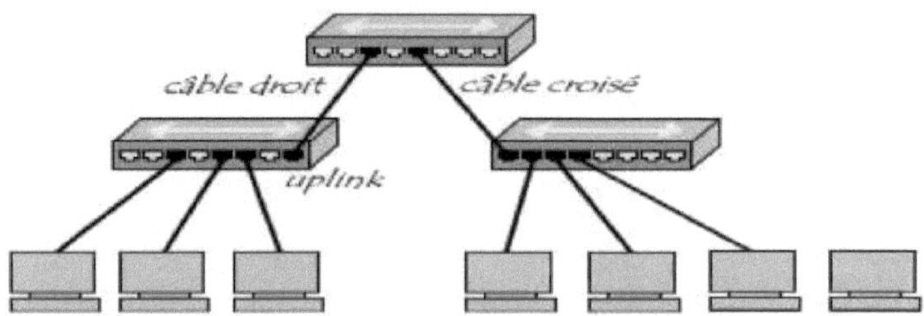

If you want to connect several machines to your Internet connection, a hub is not enough. You will need to use a router or switch, or let the computer connected directly to the connection act as a gateway (so it will always be on when the other computers on the network want to access the Internet).

4- Bridges

Bridges are hardware devices used to link networks working with the same protocol. Unlike a repeater, which works at the physical level, a bridge also works at the logical level (at layer 2 of the OSI model), i.e. it is capable of filtering frames by only letting through those whose address corresponds to a machine located on the opposite side of the bridge. In this way, the bridge enables a network to be segmented, keeping frames intended for the local network at local level and transmitting frames intended for other networks. This reduces traffic (particularly collisions) on each of the networks and increases confidentiality, as information intended for one network cannot be listened in on the other. On the other hand, the filtering operation carried out by the bridge can lead to a slight slowdown when passing from one network to another, which is why bridges must be judiciously placed in a network.

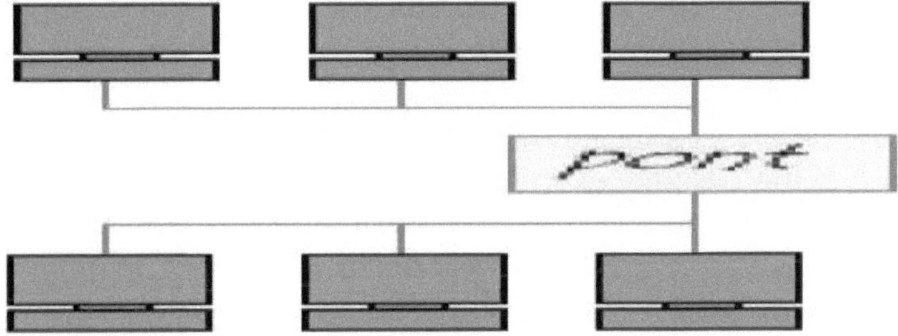

A bridge is usually used to transfer packets between two networks of the same type.

1- Principle

A bridge has two connections to two separate networks. When the bridge receives a frame on one of its interfaces, it analyses the MAC address of the recipient and the sender. If the bridge does not know the sender, it stores the address in a table in order to "remember" which side of the network the sender is on. In this way, the bridge knows whether the sender and receiver are on the same side or on opposite sides of the bridge. In the first case, the bridge ignores the message; in the second, the bridge transmits the frame to the other network.

2- Bridge operation

A bridge operates at the *Data Link* layer of the OSI model, i.e. it operates at the level of the physical addresses of the machines. In reality, the bridge is connected to several local networks, called **segments**. The bridge creates a table of correspondence between the addresses of the machines and the segment to which they belong, and "listens" to the data circulating on the segments.

During a data transmission, the bridge checks the mapping table to determine the segment to which the sending and receiving computers belong (using their physical address, known as the MAC address, and not their IP address. If they belong to the same segment, the bridge does nothing, otherwise it will switch the data to the segment to which the receiver belongs.

3- Usefulness of such a device

The bridge allows a network to be segmented, i.e. in the case shown above, communications between the 3 computers shown at the top do not clutter up the network lines between the 3 computers at the bottom, information will only pass when a computer on one side of the bridge sends data to a computer on the other side. ⁄ χ.

These bridges can also be connected to a modem, to ensure the continuity of a remote local network.

Here is a schematic diagram of a bridge:

4- The *switch* is a multi-port bridge, i.e. an active element operating at level 2 of the OSI model. The switch analyses the frames arriving on its input ports and filters the data to route them only to the appropriate ports (this is known as **switching** or **switched networks**). In other words, the switch combines the filtering properties of a bridge and the connectivity properties of a concentrator.

Here is a schematic diagram of a switch:

5- Application gateways

Application gateways are hardware and software systems used to link two networks, in particular to interface between different protocols.

When a remote user contacts such a device, it examines the request, and if it corresponds to the rules defined by the network administrator, the gateway creates a bridge between the two networks. The information is therefore not transmitted directly, but 'translated' to ensure the continuity of the two protocols.

As well as providing an interface between two heterogeneous networks, this system offers additional security, as every piece of information is scrutinised (which can cause a slowdown) and sometimes added to a log that traces the history of events. The major disadvantage of this system is that such an application must be available for each service (FTP, HTTP, Telnet, etc).

6- Routers

Presentation of routers

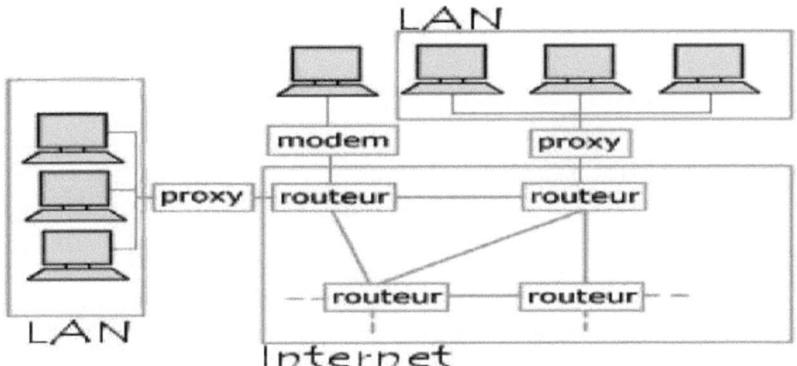

Routers are the key machines on the Internet, as it is these devices that "choose" the path that a message will take. When you request a URL, the Web client queries the DNS, which indicates the IP address of the machine in question. Your workstation sends the request to the nearest router (usually the network gateway), which chooses the next machine to which it will forward the request so that the path chosen is the shortest.

In addition, routers make it possible to manipulate data (which circulates in the form of datagrams) so that it can be passed from one type of network to another (unlike a bridge-type device). This means that the networks cannot circulate the same amount of information at the same time in terms of data packet size. Routers therefore have the ability to fragment data packets to allow them to circulate.

Lastly, some routers are capable of creating maps (routing tables) of the routes to be followed according to the target address, using protocols dedicated to this task.

1- What a router looks like

The first routers were simple computers with several network cards (known as multi-host machines), each of which was connected to a different network.

Most of today's routers are dedicated to the task of routing. A router has several network interfaces, each connected to a different network. A router therefore has as many IP addresses as there are different networks to which it is connected.

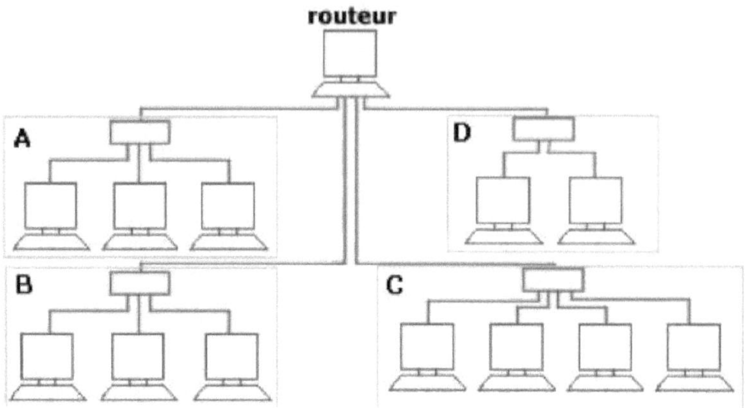

2- Types of routing

There are generally two types of routing algorithm:

· *Distance vector* routers compile a routing table listing and calculating the "cost" (in terms of the number of hops) of each route, then forward this table to neighbouring routers. Each time a connection is requested, the router chooses the "least expensive" route.

· **Link** *state* routers listen to the network continuously in order to identify the various elements surrounding it. From this information, each router calculates the shortest path (in time) to neighbouring routers and broadcasts this information in the form of *update packets*. Finally, each router builds its routing table by calculating the shortest paths to all the other routers (using *Dijkstra*'s algorithm).

3- How a router works

In the case above, the scenario is simple. If the router receives packets from network A for network B, it will simply forward the packets to network B...

However, on the Internet the scheme is much more complicated for the following reasons:

· The number of networks to which a router is connected is generally high;

· The networks to which the router is connected may be linked to other networks of which the router has no direct knowledge.

Routers operate using routing tables and routing protocols, which are explained in the routing section.

7- B-wheelers

1- Introducing B-routeurs

A *B-router* is a hybrid device combining the functions of a router and a bridge. This type of equipment enables non-routable protocols to be transferred from one network to another, while routing others. More precisely, the B-router acts primarily as a bridge and routes packets if this is not possible.

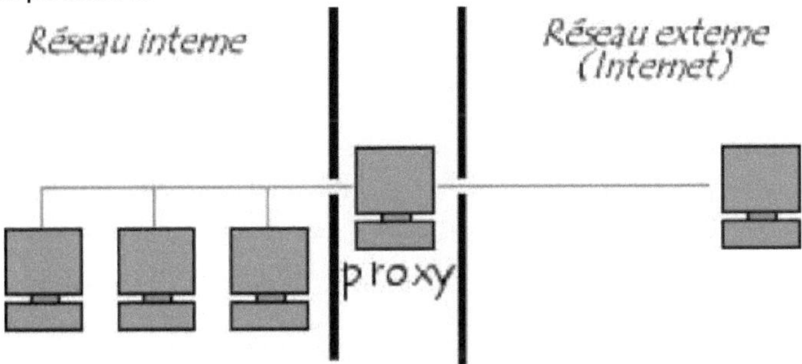

A B-router can therefore, in certain architectures, be more economical and compact than a router and a bridge.

PROXY

1-Introduction to the notion of proxy

A **proxy** *server* is a machine that acts as an intermediary between computers on a local network (sometimes using protocols other than TCP/IP) and the Internet.

Most of the time the proxy server is used for the web, in which case it is an HTTP proxy. However, there may be proxy servers for each application protocol (FTP, etc.).

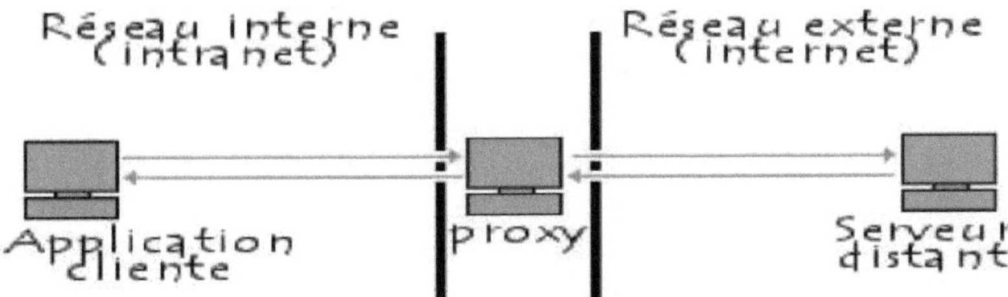

2- How a proxy works

The basic operating principle of a proxy server is quite simple: it is a server "mandated" by an application to carry out a request on the Internet on its behalf. So when a user connects to the Internet using a client application configured to use a proxy server, the client application will first connect to the proxy server and give it its request. The proxy server will then connect to the server that the client application is trying to reach and send it the request. The server will then give its response to the proxy, which will in turn pass it on to the client application.

3- Proxy server features

Now, with the use of TCP/IP within local networks, the relay role of the proxy server is performed directly by gateways and routers. However, proxy servers are still relevant today thanks to a number of other functions.

4- The cache function

Most proxies provide a *caching* function, i.e. the ability to store (*cache*) the pages most frequently visited by users of the local network so that they can be provided as quickly as possible. In computing, the term 'cache' refers to a temporary data storage space (the term 'buffer' is also sometimes used).

A proxy server with the ability to cache information is generally referred to as a "**proxy-cache** server".

This feature, which is implemented in certain proxy servers, reduces the use of bandwidth to the Internet and cuts document access times for users.

However, to carry out this mission successfully, the proxy needs to regularly compare the data it stores in cache memory with the remote data to ensure that the cached data is still valid.

5- Filtering

By using a proxy, it is also possible to monitor connections (*logging* or *tracking*) by creating activity *logs* that systematically record users' requests when they connect to the Internet.

It is therefore possible to filter Internet connections by analysing both client requests and server responses. When filtering is carried out by comparing the client's request with a list of authorised requests, this is known as a *white list*; when it is a list of prohibited sites, it is known as a *black list*. Finally, the analysis of server responses according to a list of criteria (keywords, etc.) is called *content filtering*. 6- Authentication

Insofar as the proxy is the essential intermediary for users of the internal network to access external resources, it is sometimes possible to use it to authenticate users, i.e. to ask them to identify themselves using a user name and password, for example. This makes it easy to

give access to external resources only to people authorised to do so, and be able to record identified accesses in log files.

When implemented, this type of mechanism poses a serious risk to the environment.

There are obviously many problems relating to individual freedoms and personal rights...

7- Reverse-proxy

A *reverse-proxy* server is a proxy-cache server that is "mounted in reverse", i.e. a proxy server that does not allow users to access the Internet, but rather allows Internet users to access the Internet indirectly. The reverse proxy acts as a relay for Internet users to certain internal servers.

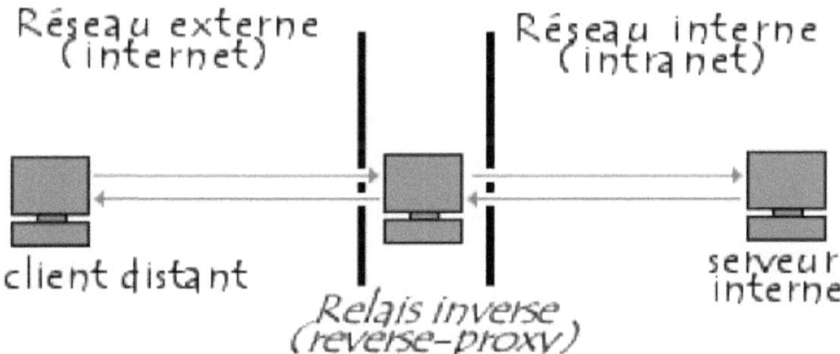

wishing to access an internal website by indirectly transmitting requests to it. Thanks to the reverse-proxy, the web server is protected from direct attacks from outside, which strengthens the security of the internal network. In addition, the reverse-proxy's caching function can relieve the load on the server for which it is intended, which is why such a server is sometimes called a "*server accelerator*".

Finally, thanks to sophisticated algorithms, the reverse proxy can be used to distribute the load by redirecting requests to different equivalent servers; this is known as "load *balancing*".

8- Setting up a proxy server

The most widely used proxy is undoubtedly Squid, an open-source program available on many platforms, including Windows and Linux.

Under Windows, there are several software packages that allow you to set up a proxy server for your local network at a lower cost:

. Wingate is the most common (but not free) solution.

. configuring a proxy with Jana server is becoming increasingly common.

. Windows 2000 incorporates Microsoft Proxy Server (MSP), supplemented by Microsoft Proxy Client, to perform this operation.

CHAPTER 5

INTERNET PROTOCOLS

1- Presentation

In the early days of computing, computers were developed and, as soon as they were capable of operating on their own, people came up with the idea of linking them together so that they could exchange data - the concept of a network. It was therefore necessary to develop physical links between computers so that information could circulate, but also a communication language so that there could be a real exchange. It was decided to name this language: *protocol*.

Numerous protocols are used on the Internet, all part of a suite of protocols known as TCP/IP. TCP/IP is based on the identification of each computer by an address called *IP address*, which enables data to be sent to the correct address. These addresses are then associated with domain names to make them easier to remember.

Heterogeneous networks (of different kinds) developed in the four corners of the globe, and people decided to link these networks together (universities, for example, or the army). Protocols evolved to enable all these networks to communicate with each other, forming a network of networks, gradually forming a gigantic spider's web - the largest network, containing all the networks, known as the **Internet**! On the Internet there are different protocols (languages used between computers) that allow different things to be done:

- IRC: chat live
- http: view web pages
- ftp: transfer files
- and much more

Each of them is assigned a number (the port) which is transmitted during communication (transmission is carried out in small packets of information). In this way, we know which programme corresponds to each small packet:

- http packets arrive on port 80 and are transmitted to the web browser from which the page was called up
- irc packets arrive on port 6667 (or another port usually around 7000) and are forwarded to a program such as mIRC (or similar).

2-Connecting to the Internet

The network card is the part of the computer that allows you to connect to a network via lines specially designed to carry digital information. The modem, on the other hand, allows you to connect to a network via telephone lines... which were not originally designed for this purpose (but which are still the most common means of communication). A network card has its own IP address (this is how you can distinguish between different computers on the Internet ... otherwise it's difficult to set up a communication system).

Connecting via a modem is completely different. A modem is used to establish communication between two computers via a telephone line. However, you can access a network (and therefore, by extension, the Internet) by contacting a computer connected ("on one side") to one or more telephone lines (to receive your call) and ("on the other side") to a network via a network card. This computer usually belongs to your Internet Service Provider (ISP). When it connects you through it, it lends you an IP address that you keep for the duration of the connection. Each time you connect, it will arbitrarily assign you one of the free IP addresses it has, so this is not a "fixed" IP address.

a-Protocols

A **protocol** is a standard method of communication between processes (possibly running on different machines), i.e. a set of rules and procedures to be followed when sending and receiving data on a network. There are several protocols, depending on what is expected of the communication. Some protocols, for example, specialise in exchanging files (FTP), while others simply manage transmission status and errors (e.g. the ICMP protocol). On the Internet, the protocols used are part of a protocol suite, i.e. a set of interconnected protocols. This protocol suite is called TCP/IP. It contains, among others, the following protocols:

. **HTTP, FTP, ARP, ICMP, IP, TCP, UDP, SMTP, Telnet, NNTP**

Connection-oriented and nonconnection-oriented protocols

Protocols are generally divided into two categories depending on the level of data control required:

. **Connection-oriented protocols**: These are protocols which control the transmission of data **during** a communication between two machines. In such a scheme, the receiving machine sends acknowledgements of receipt during the communication, so that the sending machine guarantees the validity of the data it sends. Data is sent in the form of a stream. TCP is a connection-oriented protocol

. **Non-connection-oriented protocols**: This is a communication mode in which the sending machine sends data without notifying the receiving machine, and the receiving machine receives the data without notifying

the sending machine. The data is sent in the form of blocks (datagrams).
UDP is a **non-connection-oriented** protocol

b- Protocol and implementation

A protocol defines only the way in which machines should communicate, i.e. the form and sequence of the data to be exchanged. However, a protocol does not define how to program software so that it is compatible with the protocol. **Implementation** is the translation of a protocol into computer language.

Protocol specifications are never exhaustive, so it is common for implementations to be subject to a certain interpretation of the specifications, which sometimes leads to specificities in certain implementations or worse to incompatibilities or security flaws c- IP address

What is an IP address

On the Internet, computers communicate with each other using the TCP/IP protocol, which uses <u>32-bit</u> numbers, written in the form of 4 numbers from 0 to 255 (4 times 8 bits), in the form xxx.xxx.xxx.xxx where each xxx represents an integer from 0 to 255. These numbers are used by computers on the network to identify each other, so that no two computers on the network have the same IP address (IP stands for *Internet Protocol*).

For example, *194.153.205.26* is a TCP/IP address given in technical form. These are the addresses known by the computers that communicate with them.

IANA (*Internet Assigned Numbers Agency*) is responsible for assigning these numbers.

Decrypting an IP address

As we have seen, an IP address is a 32-bit address written as 4 integers separated by dots. There are actually two parts to an IP address:

•   part of the numbers on the left identifies the network (this is called *netID*)

•   The numbers on the right identify the computers on this network (called *host-ID*).

Let's take an example:

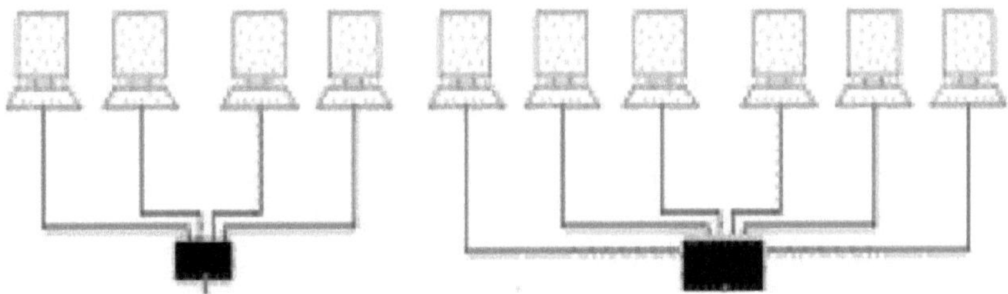

Hterne is represented above by two small networks.
The network on the left is 194.28.12. It contains the following computers:
.   194.28.12.1 à 194.28.12.4
The one on the right is 178.12.77. It will include the following computers:
.   178.12.77.1 à 178.12.77.6
The networks are therefore numbered 194.28.12 and 178.12.77, then each of the computers in the network is numbered incrementally. Imagine a large network numbered *58.24*: the computers connected to it will generally be given IP addresses ranging from *58.24.0.1* to *58.24.255.254*. So the numbers have to be allocated in such a way that there is an organisation in the hierarchy of computers and servers...
The smaller the number of bits reserved for the network, the more computers it can contain. In fact, a network rated 102 can contain computers with IP addresses ranging from 102.0.0.1 to 102.255.255.254
    (256*256*256-2=16777214 possibilities), while
that a network noted 194.26 can only contain computers whose IP address is between 194.26.0.1 and 194.26.255.254 (256*256-2=65534 possibilities), this is the notion of **class**.
Special addresses
When the host-id part is cancelled, i.e. when the bits reserved for the network machines are replaced, we obtain what is known as the **network address**.
For example, 194.28.12.0 is a network address and so cannot be assigned to any of the computers on the network.
When the netid part is cancelled, i.e. when the bits reserved for the network are replaced, we obtain what is known as the **machine address**. This address represents the machine specified by the host-ID on the current network.
When all the bits in the host-id part are set to 1, we obtain what is known as the **broadcast address**, i.e. an address that will be used to send the message to all the machines on the network specified by the *netID*.
When all the bits in the netid part are set to 1, we obtain what is known

as the **multicast address**.

The address **127.0.0.1** is known as the **loopback address**, because it refers to the local *host*.

3- Network classes

IP addresses are therefore divided into classes, according to the number of bytes representing the network.

Class A

In a class A IP address, the first byte represents the network. The most significant bit (the first bit, on the left) is zero, which means that there are 2^7 (00000000 to 01111111) possible networks, i.e. 128. However, network 0 (00000000)

does not exist and the number 127 is reserved to designate your machine, so the networks available in class A are those from **1.0.0.0** to **126.0.0.0** (when the last bytes are zeros this indicates a network and not a computer!)

The three bytes on the right represent the network computers, so the network can contain: 2^{24} - 2 = 16777214 computers.

A Class A IP address, in binary, looks like this:

0	**XXXXXXX**	*XXXXXXXX*	<u>XXXXXXXX</u>	XXXXXXXX
	Network		Computers	

Class B

In a class B IP address, the first two octets represent the network. The first two bits are 1 and 0, which means that there are 2^{14} (10 000000 00000000 to 10 111111 11111111) possible networks, i.e. 16384. The two bytes on the right represent the computers on the network, so the network can contain: 2^{16} - 2^1 = 65534 computers.

A Class B IP address, in binary, looks like this:

10	XXXXXX	XXXXXXXX	XXXXXXXX	XXXXXXXX
	Network		Computers	

Class C

In a class C IP address, the first three octets represent the network. The first three bits are 1, 1 and 0, which means that there are $2{,}^{21}$ possible networks, i.e. 2097152. The networks available in class C are therefore those from **192.0.0.0** to **223.255.255.0.**

The byte on the right represents the computers on the network, so the network can contain: 2^8 - 2^1 = 254 computers.

A class C IP address, in binary, looks like this:

110	xxxxx	xxxxxxxx	xxxxxxxx	xxxxxxxx
	Network			Computers

Allocation of IP addresses

The purpose of dividing IP addresses into three classes A, B and C is to make it easier to find a computer on the network. Using this notation, you can first search for the network you want to reach and then search for a computer on that network. IP addresses are allocated according to the size of the network.

Class	Number of possible networks	Maximum number of computers on each
A	126	16 777 214
B	16 384	65 534
C	2 097152	254

Class A addresses are reserved for very large networks, while Class C addresses are allocated to small corporate networks, for example Reserved IP addresses

It often happens in a company that only one computer is connected to the Internet, and it is through this computer that the other computers on the network access the Internet (this is generally referred to as a proxy). In this case, only the computer connected to the Internet needs to reserve an IP address with the INTERNIC.

However, the other computers still need an IP address to be able to communicate with each other internally. INTERNIC has therefore reserved a handful of addresses in each class so that computers on a local network connected to the Internet can be assigned an IP address without the risk of creating IP address conflicts on the network. These are the following addresses: .   10.0.0.1 à 10.255.255.254

.   172.16.0.1 à 172.31.255.254

.   192.168.0.1 à 192.168.255.254

Subnet masks

Notion of mask

To understand what a mask is, it may be interesting to have a look at the assembler section which talks about binary masking. To summarise, we create a mask containing 1s in the places of the bits we want to keep, and 0s for those we want to make equal to zero. Once this mask has been created, all you have to do is AND the value you want to mask with the mask to keep the part you want intact and cancel the rest.

A network mask (*netmask*) takes the form of 4 bytes separated by dots (like an IP address), and includes (in its binary notation) zeros for the bits of the IP address you want to delete (and 1s for the bits you want to keep).

Benefits of a mask

There are in fact several. One of them is to know the network associated with an IP address.

As we saw earlier, the network is determined by a certain number of bytes in the IP address (1 byte for class A addresses, 2 for class B addresses and 3 bytes for class C). In addition, we have seen that a network is scored by taking the number of bytes that characterise it, then adding 0s.

For example, the network associated with the address *34.56.123.12* is *34.0.0.0* (since this is a class A address). To find out the address of the network associated with the IP address 34.56.123.12, all you need to do is apply a mask where the first byte only contains 1's (which gives 255), then 0's on the following bytes (which gives 0..).

The mask is: *11111111.00000000.00000000.00000000*

The mask associated with the IP address *34.208.123.12* is therefore *255.0.0.0*.

The binary value of *34.208.123.12* is:

00100010.11010000.01111011.00001100

One and between

00100010.11010000.01111011.00001100

and

11111111.00000000.00000000.00000000 donne

00100010.00000000.00000000.00000000

i.e. *34.0.0.0*, which is the network associated with the address *34.208.123.12.*

By generalising, we obtain the following masks for each class:

. For a **Class A** address, we are only interested in the first byte, so we have a mask of the form *11111111.00000000.00000000.*00000000, i.e. in decimal notation: **255.0.0.0**

. For a **Class B** address, we are interested in the first two bytes, so we have a mask of the form *11111111.11111111.00000000.*00000000, i.e. in decimal notation: **255.255.0.0**

. For a **Class C** address

We are interested in the first three bytes, so we have a mask of the form *11111111.11111111.11111111.*00000000, i.e. in decimal notation:

255.255.255.0

Creating sub-networks

Let's go back to the example of the 34.0.0.0 network, and suppose we want the first two bits of the second byte to be used to designate the network.

The mask to be applied will then be:

11111111.11000000.00000000.00000000 i.e. 255.192.0.0

If we apply this mask to the address 34.208.123.12 we get: 34.192.0.0

In reality, there are 4 possible scenarios for the result of masking the IP address of a computer on the 34.0.0.0 network

- Either the first two bits of the second byte are **00**, in which case the masking result is **255.0.0.0**
- Either the first two bits of the second byte are **01**, in which case the masking result is **255.64.0.0**
- Either the first two bits of the second byte are **10**, in which case the masking result is **255.128.0.0**
- The first two bits of the second byte are **11**, in which case the masking result is **255.192.0.0**

This masking therefore divides a class A network (capable of admitting 16777214 computers) into 4 sub-networks (hence the name *sub-network mask*) capable of admitting 2^{22} computers, i.e. 4194304 computers.

Incidentally, the total number of possible computers in both cases is 16777214 (4 x 4194304 - 2 = 16777214).

The number of subnets depends on the number of extra bits assigned to the network (here).

The number of sub-networks is therefore

Number of bits	Number of sub-networks
1	2
2	4
3	8
4	16
5	32
6	64
7	128
8 (impossible for a C class)	256

4-The Domain Name System

1- The Domain Name System (DNS)

Every computer that is directly connected to the Internet has at least one IP address of its own. However, users do not want to work with numerical addresses such as *194.153.205.26*, but with machine names or more explicit addresses (called FQDN addresses) such as http://www.commentcamarche.net/.

It is therefore possible to associate names in everyday language with numerical addresses thanks to a system called **DNS** (*Domain Name System*).

Domain name resolution (or *address resolution*) is the correlation between IP addresses and the associated domain name.

Host names

In the early days of TCP/IP, because networks were very small, or in other words the number of computers connected to a single network was small, network administrators created files called *manual translation tables*. These manual conversion tables were sequential files, generally called *hosts* or *hosts.txt*, associating on each line the IP address of the machine and the associated literal name, called the *host name*.

2- Introduction to the Domain Name System

However, the previous system of conversion tables required the tables on all computers to be updated manually whenever a machine name was added or changed. So, with the explosion in the size of networks and their interconnections, a hierarchical, more easily administered name management system had to be put in place. The **Domain** *Name System* (**DNS**) was developed in November 1983 by Paul Mockapetris (RFC 882 and RFC 883), then revised in 1987 in RFCs 1034 and 1035. The DNS has since been the subject of numerous RFCs.

This system offers :

•   a hierarchical **namespace** that guarantees the uniqueness of a name in a tree structure, in the same way as Unix file systems.

•   a system of **distributed servers** to make the name space available.

•   a **client** system for 'resolving' domain names, i.e. querying servers to find out the IP address corresponding to a name.

The namespace

The structure of the DNS system is based on a tree structure in which top-level domains are defined.

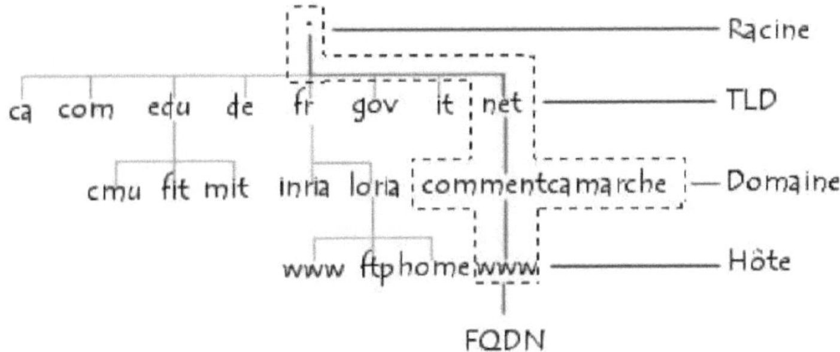

(called **TLDs**, for *Top Level Domains*), attached to a root node represented by a dot.

Each node in the tree is called a "**domain name**". Each node has a *label* of up to 63 characters.

All the domain names together form an inverted tree, with each node separated from the next by a dot ("."). The end of a branch is called the **host**, and corresponds to a machine or network entity. The host name assigned to it must be unique in the domain in question, or in the sub-domain if applicable. For example, the web server of a domain generally bears the name *www*. The word "**domain**" formally corresponds to the suffix of a domain name, i.e. all the node labels of a tree, with the exception of the host.

The absolute name corresponding to all the labels of the nodes of a tree, separated by dots and ending with a full stop, is called an **FQDN** (*Fully Qualified Domain Name*) **address**. The maximum depth of the tree is 127 levels and the maximum length of an FQDN name is 255 characters. The FQDN address is used to uniquely identify a machine on the network of networks. For example, *www.commentcamarche.net* represents an FQDN address.

3- Name servers

Machines known as *domain name servers* are used to establish the correspondence between the domain name and the IP address of machines on a network.

Each domain has a domain name server, called the primary *domain name server*, and a secondary *domain name server*, which takes over from the primary name server if it is unavailable.

Each name server is declared in a domain name server of the level immediately above, which implicitly allows delegation of authority over domains. The name system is a distributed architecture, where each entity is responsible for managing its own domain name. There is therefore no single organisation responsible for managing all domain names. The servers corresponding to the Top Level Domains (TLDs) are called "**root name servers**". There are thirteen of these, spread around the world, with the names "a.root- servers.net" to "m.root-servers.net".

A name server defines a zone, i.e. a set of domains over which the server has authority. The *domain name* system is transparent to the user, but the following points should not be forgotten:

•   Each computer must be configured with the address of a machine capable of transforming any name into an IP address. This machine is called a Domain Name Server. Don't panic: when you connect to the Internet, your ISP will automatically modify your network settings to make these name servers available to you.

•   The IP address of a second *Domain Name Server* (secondary Domain Name Server) must also be defined: the secondary name server can relay the primary name server in the event of a malfunction.

The most common server is called **BIND** (*Berkeley Internet Name Domain*).

This is a free software application available on UNIX systems, initially developed by the University of Berkeley in California and now maintained by the *ISC* (*Internet Systems Consortium*).

4- Domain name resolution

The process of finding the IP address corresponding to the name of a host is called "domain name resolution". The application that performs this operation (usually integrated into the operating system) is called a "*resolver*". When an application wishes to connect to a host known by its domain name (for example www.commentcamarche.net), it queries a name server defined in its network configuration. Each machine connected to the network has in its configuration the IP addresses of two name servers belonging to its access provider.

A request is sent to the ISP's first name server. If it has the record in its cache, it sends it to the application, otherwise it queries a root server (in our case a root server corresponding to the ".net" TLD). This root server will in turn return the IP address of the authoritative name server for the domain (in our case it will return the IP addresses of the two *commentcamarche.net* name servers).

The primary name server with authority over the domain will then be queried and will return the record corresponding to the host on the domain (in our case *www*).

5-Recording types

A DNS is a distributed database containing records, called **RRs** (*Resource Records*), relating to domain names. The information below can only be read by those responsible for administering a domain, as the operation of name servers is completely transparent to users.

Because of the caching system that allows the DNS system to be distributed, the records for each domain have a lifetime, called **TTL** (*Time To Live*), which allows the intermediate servers to know when the information has expired and whether or not it needs to be re-checked.

Generally speaking, a DNS record contains the following information:

Domain name (FQDN)	TTL	Type	Class	RData
www.commentcamarche.net.	3600	A	IN	163.5.255.85

- **Domain name**: the domain name must be an FQDN name, i.e. it must end with a dot. If the dot is omitted, the domain name is relative, i.e. the main domain name will suffix the domain entered;
- **Type**: a 16-bit value specifying the type of resource described by the record. The resource type can be one of the following:
  - **A**: this is the basic type establishing the correspondence between a canonical name and an IP address. There may also be several A records, corresponding to different machines on the network (servers).
  - **CNAME** (*CanonicalName*): this allows you to make match an alias to the canonical name. It is particularly useful for providing alternative names for different services on the same machine.
  - **HINFO**: this is a purely descriptive field used to describe the hardware (CPU) and operating system (OS) of a host. It is generally advisable to leave this field blank so as not to provide information that could be useful to hackers.
  - **MX** (*Mail eXchange*): corresponds to the mail management server. When a user sends an e-mail to an address (user@domain), the outgoing mail server queries the name server with authority over the domain to obtain the MX record. There may be several MX records per domain, to provide redundancy in the event of failure of the main mail server. The MX record can be used to define a priority with a value ranging from 0 to 65 535: www.commentcamarche.net. IN MX 10 mail.commentcamarche.net.
  - **NS**: corresponds to the name server with authority over the domain.
  - **PTR**: a pointer to another part of the

domain names.

- ○ **SOA** (*Start Of Authority*): the SOA field is used to
describe the name server with authority over the zone, as well as the technical contact's e-mail address (where the "@" character is replaced by a full stop).
- · **Class**: the class can be either **IN** (corresponding to Internet protocols, so this is the system used in our case) or **CH** (for the chaotic system);
- · **RDATA**:   this is the data corresponding to
the recording. The information required depends on the type of record:
- ○ A: a 32-bit IP address ;
- ○ CNAME: a ;
- ○ MX: a 16-bit priority value, followed by a host name ;
- ○ NS: a host name ;
- ○ PTR: a ;
- ○ SOA: several fields.

5- High-level domains

There are two categories of **TLD** (*Top Level Domain*):

Generic" domains, known as **gTLDs** (*generic TLDs*). gTLDs are generic top-level domain names classified according to sector of activity. Each gTLD has its own access rules:

- ○ historical gTLDs :
- ▪ **.arpa** corresponds to machines from the original network ;
- ▪ **.com** initially corresponded to commercial companies. This TLD has now become the "default TLD" and the acquisition of domains with this extension is possible, including by private individuals.
- ▪ **.edu** corresponds to educational organisations;
- ▪ **.gov** corresponds to government agencies
- ▪ **.int** corresponds to international organisations ;
- ▪ **.mil** corresponds to military organisations ;
- ▪ **.net** initially corresponded to network-related organisations. In recent years, this TLD has become a common TLD. It is now possible for private individuals to acquire domains with this extension.
- ▪ **.org** usually corresponds to not-for-profit companies.
- ○ new gTLDs introduced in November 2000 by ICANN :
- ▪ **.aero** corresponds to the aeronautics industry;
- ▪ **.biz** (*business*) corresponding to commercial companies ;
- ▪ **.museum** corresponds to museums ;
- ▪ **.name** corresponds to the names of people or imaginary characters ;
- ▪ **.info** corresponds to organisations dealing with information ;

- **.coop** corresponding to cooperatives ;
- **.pro** corresponding to the liberal professions.
o special gTLDs :
- **.arpa** corresponds to network management infrastructures. The arpa gTLD is used for reverse resolution of network machines, enabling the name corresponding to an IP address to be found.
- National" domains, known as **ccTLDs** (country code TLDs). The ccTLDs correspond to the different countries and their names correspond to the abbreviations of country names defined by the ISO 3166 standard. The table below summarises the list of ccTLDs.

6- Notion of Ports

Many TCP/IP programs can be run simultaneously on the Internet (for example, you can open several browsers simultaneously or browse HTML pages while downloading a file via FTP). Each of these programs works with a protocol, but the computer must be able to distinguish between the different data sources.

To facilitate this process, each of these applications is allocated a unique address on the machine, coded on 16 bits: **a port** (the *IP address* + *port* combination is then a unique address in the world, it is called a socket).

The IP address is therefore used to uniquely identify a computer on the network, while the port number indicates the application for which the data is intended. In this way, when the computer receives information destined for a port, the data is sent to the corresponding application. If it is a request to the application, the application is called the **server** application. If it is a response, it is called a **client** application.

7- The multiplexing function

The process of being able to pass information from different applications over a connection is called multiplexing. Similarly, the process of paralleling (i.e. distributing) the data flow between different applications is called **demultiplexing**.

Machine   AMMachine B

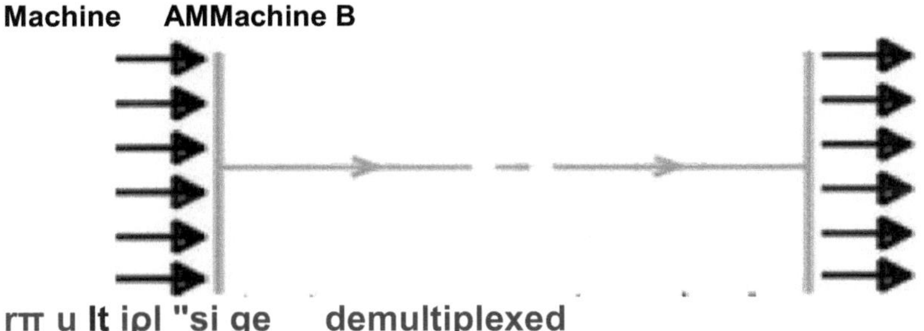

These operations are carried out using a port, i.e. a number associated with a type of application, which, combined with an IP address, makes it possible to uniquely identify an application running on a given machine. Default assignments.

There are thousands of ports (these are coded on 16 bits, so there are 65536 possibilities), which is why a standard assignment has been developed by the **IANA** (*Internet Assigned Numbers Authority*) to help configure networks.

•	Ports 0 to 1023 are "**Well Known Ports**". They are generally reserved for system processes (daemons) or programs.

executed by privileged users. A network administrator can, however, bind services to the ports of his choice.

•	Ports 1024 to 49151 are called "**Registered Ports**".

•	Ports 49152 to 65535 are "**Dynamic and/or Private Ports**".

Here are some of the most commonly used recognised ports:

Port	Service or Application
21	FTP
23	Telnet
25	SMTP
53	Domain Name System
63	Whois
70	Gopher
79	Finger
80	HTTP
110	POP3
119	NNTP

For example, a server (a computer that is contacted and offers services such as FTP, Telnet, etc.) has fixed port numbers to which the network administrator has associated services. A server's ports are generally between 0 and 1023 (a range of values associated with known services). On the client side, the port is chosen at random from those available in the operating system. For example, client ports will never be between 0 and 1023, as this range of values represents *known ports*.

8- URL

A **URL** (*Uniform Resource Locator*) is a universal naming format for a resource on the Internet. It is a string of printable ASCII characters divided into five parts:

.	**The name of the protocol**: in other words, the language used to communicate on the network. The most widely used protocol is HTTP (*HyperText Transfer Protocol*), the protocol used to exchange Web pages in HTML format. However, many other protocols can be used (FTP, News, Mailto, Gopher, etc.).

- **Username and password**: used to specify the parameters for accessing a secure server. This option is not recommended because the password is visible in the URL
- **The server name**: This is the domain name of the computer hosting the requested resource. Note that it is possible to use the server's IP address, but this makes the URL less readable.
- **Port number**: this is a number associated with a service, enabling the server to know what type of resource is being requested. The default port associated with the protocol is port number 80. So when the server's Web service is associated with port number 80, the port number is optional.
- **The access path to the resource**: This last part tells the server where the resource is located, i.e. generally the location (directory) and name of the file requested.

A URL therefore has the following structure:

Protocol	Password (optional)	Name of Server	Port (optional if 80)	Chemin
http://	user:password@	www.commentc amarche.net	: 80	/glossair/glos sair.php3

The following protocols, for example, can be used via the URL:
- http, for viewing web pages
- ftp, for consulting FTP sites
- telnet, to connect to a remote terminal
- mailto, to send an e-mail
- wais
- gopher

The filename in the URL may be followed by a question mark and then by data in ASCII format. This is additional data sent as a parameter to an application on the server (a CGI script, for example). The URL will then look like a character string like this: http://www.commentcamarche.net/forum/index.php3?cat=1&page=2

Coding a URL

Given that the URL is a means of sending information across the Internet (to send data to a CGI script, for example), it is necessary to be able to send special characters, and URLs cannot contain special characters. In addition, certain characters are reserved because they have a meaning (the slash is used to specify a sub-directory, the & and ? characters are used to send data via forms, etc.). Finally, URLs can be included in an HTML document, which makes it difficult to insert characters such as < or > in the URL.

This is why coding is necessary! Encoding consists of replacing special characters with the % character (which also becomes a special character) followed by the ASCII code of the character to be encoded in hexadecimal notation.

CHAPTER 6

INTERNET TECHNOLOGY

1- Modem

Morse code was the first coding system to enable long-distance communication. It was *Samuel F.B. Morse* who developed it in 1844. This code is made up of dots and dashes (a binary language of sorts...). It enabled much faster communications than the Pony Express. At the time, the interpreter was a human being, so a good knowledge of the code was essential...

Numerous codes were invented, including the Emile Baudot Code (also known as the *Baudot* Code, the English called it the *Murray Code*).

On 10 March 1876, Dr Graham Bell developed the telephone, a revolutionary invention that allowed voice information to be transmitted over metal lines. Incidentally, the House of Representatives decided that Antonio Meucci was responsible for inventing the telephone. He had applied for a patent in 1871, but was unable to finance it beyond 1874.

These lines led to the development of teletypewriters, machines that encoded and decoded characters using the Baudot code (characters were then encoded on 5 bits, so there were only 32 characters...).

In the 1960s, the ASCII code (American Standard Code for Information Interchange) was adopted as the standard. It allows characters to be encoded on 8 bits, giving a total of 256 possible characters.

With the advent of digitisation and modulation techniques around 1962, and the development of computers and communications, data transfer via modem was born...

2- Modem principle

The modem is the device used to transfer information between several computers (basically 2) via telephone lines. Computers work digitally, using binary language (a series of zeros and ones), but modems are analogue. Digital signals go from one value to another, there is no middle, no half, it's all or nothing (one or zero). Analogue signals, on the other hand, do not change in steps; they cover all values. So you can have 0, 0.1, 0.2, 0.3 ... 1.0 and all the values in between.

A piano, for example, works more or less 'digitally' because there are no 'steps' between the notes. A violin, on the other hand, can modulate its notes to pass through all the possible frequencies.

A computer works like a piano, a modem like a violin. The modem converts binary information from the computer into analogue. It then sends this new code down the telephone line. You can hear strange noises if you turn up the sound coming from the modem.

In this way, the modem modulates digital information into analogue waves; in the opposite direction, it retranslates data in analogue form into digital data .

That's why modem stands for MOdulateur/DEModulateur.

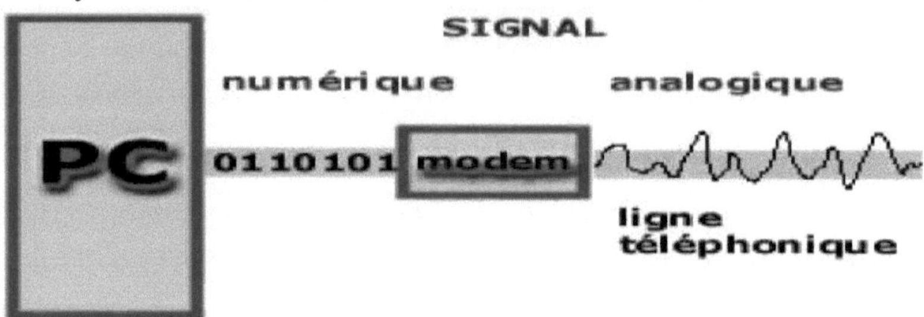

Connection via the telephone line

A telephone line is designed to work with a telephone, which is why a modem needs to establish communication with a remote computer using a telephone number before it can exchange information. A protocol is the language used by computers to communicate with each other. The two most commonly used protocols are:

- PPP protocol
- the SLIP protocol

3- The V90k MODEM(- 56FLEX)

56 Kbps modems

Rockwell has introduced a new standard: the K56flex standard. This standard is an alternative to US ROBOTICS' X2 technology.

It enables speeds of the order of 56Kb/s to be achieved over an asynchronous link. It differs in terms of encoding and server.

The average data rate is 50 Kbps, but the company is aiming for rates of around 110 and then 230 Kbps for data with a high compression ratio.

Initially, the two standards were supposed to be able to evolve.

Standards have been set since 1998. As a result, most modems offer a "flashable" bios (i.e. a modem that can be upgraded). Thanks to the V90 standard, 56 Kbps modems should now be compatible with each other.

4- ISDN/ISDN

Numeris is the commercial name of *France Telecom*'s telephone network based on **ISDN** (*Integrated Services Digital Network*) technology.

This network is designed to carry data (voice, images, faxes, etc.) separately from signalling information. ISDN owes its name to the additional services it makes possible:

- presentation of the issue
- three-way conversation
- call signal
- call forwarding
- indication of communication costs . .

In addition, ISDN provides a guaranteed 64 kbps, offering the reliability and comfort that are essential for uses requiring a high quality of service.

5- How ISDN works

You need an adapter (**TNA**, *Terminal Numérique d'Abonné*) to connect to the Numéris network. The speed is 64 Kbps (128 using two channels) instead of 56 Kbps with the fastest modems.

6- Leased lines: $T1$, $T2$, $T3$, $T4$

Leased lines are specialised lines (sometimes referred to as **LS**) that allow data to be transmitted at medium and high speeds (64 Kbps to 140 Mbps) on a point-to-point or multipoint basis (Transfix service).

In Europe, there are five types of line, depending on their speed:

. E0 (64Kbps)

. E1 = 32 EO lines (2Mbps)

. E2 = 128 lines E0 (8Mbps)

. E3 = 16 E1 lines (34Mbps)

. E4 = 64 E1 lines (140Mbps)

In the United States, the rating is as follows:

. *T1* (1.544 Mbps)

. *T2* = 4 T1 lines (6 Mbps)

. *T3* = 28 T1 lines (45 Mbps).

. *T4* = 168 T1 lines (275 Mbps).

To obtain an Internet connection, you generally need to pay a subscription fee to an Internet service provider or an online service. The price of this connection depends on the data transfer speed.

7- The Internet Link Cable

Cable Internet connections allow you to stay permanently connected to the Internet. There's no need to wait for the connection to be established with the service provider, because the connection is direct. It is already available in many French cities (Paris, Lyon, Nice, Le Mans, Annecy, Strasbourg, etc.).

The benefits:

- You don't pay for a connection by the minute, but by the month, which means lower costs.

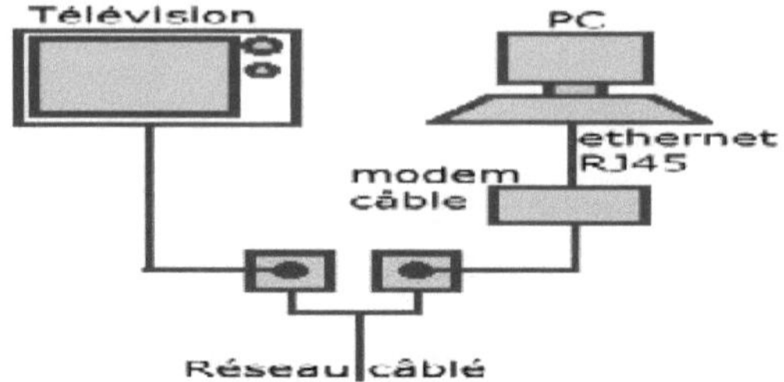

- The speed is far superior to that of a modem ...

The equipment needed for a cable link

To access this technology, you need to have:

- The cable
- An access provider via this cable
- A cable modem.

A cable modem is a device for accessing the Internet via the cable network.

It has two types of connection: a coaxial connection (to the cable) and an Ethernet RJ45 connection (to the computer's network card).

Speeds of 10Mbps can theoretically be achieved, but this bandwidth is shared according to the tree structure that connects you to the operator, so you may be (and probably are) sharing your bandwidth with everyone in your building, i.e. if all your neighbours are downloading videos, performance won't be up to scratch...

8- Clarification of the terms xDSL and ADSL?

The term **DSL** or **xDSL** stands for *Digital Subscriber Line* and brings together all the technologies used for the digital transport of information over a simple telephone connection line. XDSL technologies are divided into two main families: those using symmetrical transmission and those using asymmetrical transmission. These two families will be described later in this document.

ADSL stands for *Asymmetric Digital Subscriber Line* (in French-speaking countries this term is sometimes replaced by *LNPA*, which stands for *Ligne Numérique à Paire Asymétrique*). This system allows a high-speed downstream channel, a medium-speed upstream channel and a telephony channel (called **POTS** in telecommunications, which stands for Plain Old Telephone Service) to coexist on the same line.

9- The usefulness of xDSL and ADSL technologies

The rapid development of information technologies has led to the emergence of new services requiring large amounts of transmission capacity. Fast Internet access, videoconferencing, network interconnection, teleworking, TV programme distribution, etc. are all part of these new multimedia services that users want to obtain at home or in the office. Until now, existing high-speed services (coaxial cable, optical fibre) have not been well suited to real needs (cabling too expensive to replace with optical fibre or unstable coaxial cable connection). The idea of using twisted pair seems to be the most appropriate, since more than 800 million connections of this type are already in place around the world, and all that's needed to access ADSL is to add a piece of equipment to the telephone exchange and a small installation at the user's home.

Characteristics of ADSL technologies

The term **DSL** or **xDSL** can be broken down into several groups: HDSL, SDSL, ADSL, RADSL, VDSL. Each of these groups has its own specific use and characteristics. The differences between these technologies are as follows:

- Transmission speed
- Maximum transmission distance
- The variation in throughput between the upstream and downstream flows
- The symmetrical or non-symmetrical nature of the bond

The point-to-point connection is made via a telephone line between two pieces of equipment, the NT (Network Termination) installed on the user's premises and the LT (Line Termination) installed in the connection centre.

Symmetrical solutions

The connection is made via twisted pairs with an identical speed for both upload and download. **HDSL** (*High bit rate DSL*) is the first technology to be derived from DSL and was introduced in the early 1990s.

This technique consists of dividing the digital trunk of the network, T1 in America and **E1** in Europe, over 2 pairs of wires for T1 and 3 pairs of wires for E1. With this technique, it is possible to achieve a data rate of 2 Mbps in both directions over three twisted pairs and 1.5 Mbps in both directions over two twisted pairs. It is possible that the speed, if it is 2 Mbps, could fall to 384 kbps seconds, for example, depending on the quality of the line and the distance of the line over the last kilometre (between 3 and 7 km depending on the diameter of the wire, between 0.4mm and 0.8mm respectively).

The connection can be permanent, but there is no telephony channel available with an HDSL connection.

The current problem with this technology is that it is not yet fully standardised. **SDSL** (*Single pair DSL*, or *symmetric DSL*) is the precursor to HDSL2 (this technology, derived from HDSL, should offer the same performance as HDSL but over a single twisted pair). This technique is

designed for shorter distances than HDSL (see table below). SDSL technology is likely to disappear in favour of HDSL2.

Downstream : [Kbit/s]	Upstream : [Kbit/s]	Distance : [km]
128	128	7
256	256	6.5
384	384	4.5
768	768	4
1024	1024	3.5
2048	2048	3

Distances and speeds of an SDSL link

Asymmetrical solutions

By studying different scenarios, we realised that it was possible to transmit data more quickly from an exchange to a user, but that when the user sends information to the exchange, they are more sensitive to noise caused by electromagnetic interference (the closer you get to the exchange, the greater the concentration of cables, so they generate more crosstalk).

The idea is therefore to use an asymmetric system, imposing a lower speed from the subscriber to the exchange.

ADSL (*Asymmetric Digital Subscriber Line*), like HDSL, has existed for around ten years and was initially developed to receive television over the traditional telephone network. But the development of the Internet has given this technology a new function, enabling people to surf the net quickly without using a telephone line. ADSL is also currently one of the only technologies available on the market that offers the transport of TV/video in digital form (MPEG1 or MPEG 2) using a telephone connection. ADSL also supports TCP/IP, ATM and X.25 data transport.

The ADSL standard was finalised in 1995 and includes :

. One telephone channel with analogue or ISDN connection

. An uplink channel with a maximum capacity of 800 kbits/s

. A downlink channel with a maximum data rate of 8192 kbits/s

As with all DSL technologies, the loop distance between the exchange and the user must not exceed certain ranges in order to guarantee good data throughput (see table).

Downstream:[Kbit/s]	Upstream:[Kbit/s]	wire diameter: [Mm]	Distance: [km]
2048	160	0.4	3.6
2048	160	0.5	4.9
4096	384	0.4	3.3
4096	384	0.5	4.3
6144	640	0.4	3.0
6144	640	0.5	4.0
8192	800	0.4	2.4
8192	800	0.5	3.3

Flow rates as a function of distance and cable diameter

For data transmission, two modulation techniques have been used by ADSL equipment manufacturers:

. **CAP** (*Carrierless Amplitude and Phase Modulation*) is a variant of QAM (Quadratic Amplitude Modulation) technology. Widely used at the start of the ADSL era, this type of modulation has never been properly standardised and, as a result, there is no possible interoperability between equipment made by different manufacturers.

. **DMT** (*Discrete Multi Tone*) is a more recent modulation technique. Its principle is based on the use of a large number of sub-carriers distributed over the frequency band used by the system (see "ADSL modulation techniques"). This diagram shows the various functional blocks that make up an ADSL link.

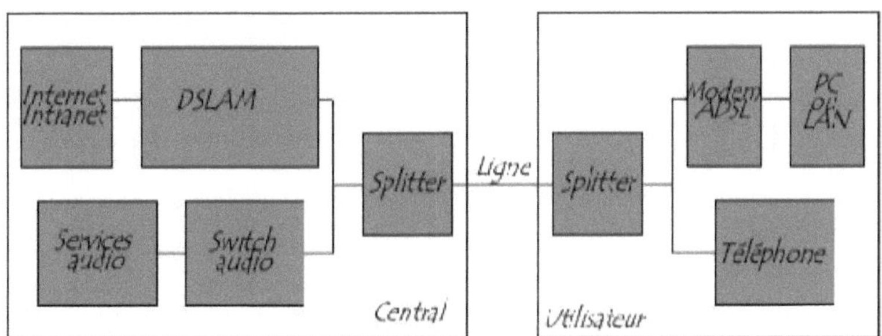

The 2 service categories are separated in the network and at the customer's premises by a splitter.

At the end of 1998, the **ITU** (*International Telecommunications Union*) standardised a new standard: **ADSL-Lite**, which is in fact a lighter version of ADSL. ADSL-Lite has a lower data rate than its predecessor (around 1.5 Mbit/s) and does not require a splitter.

RADSL (Rate Adaptive DSL) technology is based on ADSL. The transmission speed is set automatically and dynamically by seeking the maximum possible speed on the connection line and readjusting it continuously and without interruption.

RADSL would allow uplink speeds of 128kbps to 1Mbps and downlink speeds of 600kbps to 7Mbps, for a maximum local loop length of 5.4km. RADSL uses DMT modulation (as does ADSL for the most part). It is currently being standardised by ANSI.

VDSL (*Very High Bit Rate DSL*) is the fastest of the DSL technologies and is based on RADSL. It is capable of supporting, on a single twisted pair, speeds of 13 to 55.2 Mbps downstream and 1.5 to 6 Mbps upstream or, if you want to use it as a symmetrical connection, a speed of 34 Mbps in both directions. VDSL can be used as an asymmetrical or symmetrical connection.

VDSL was mainly developed for transporting high-speed **ATM** (*Asynchronous Transfer Mode*) over short distances (up to 1.5 km).

The standard is currently being standardised. QAM, CAP, DMT, DWMT (Discrete Wavelet MultiTone) and SLC (Simple Line Code) modulations are being studied.

For data transport, the VDSL equipment is connected to the central office by optical fibres forming 155 Mbps, 622 Mbps or 2.5 Gbps SDH loops. Voice traffic between the VDSL equipment and the central office can also be carried over copper lines. How to combine an analogue and ADSL network on the same line Description of a copper cable

The twisted pair consists of two copper conductors with a diameter of between 0.4mm and 0.8mm (rarely 1mm). The conductors are insulated and twisted to reduce crosstalk. Most of the time, the twisted pairs are grouped into four in a cable protected by a plastic jacket. Cables

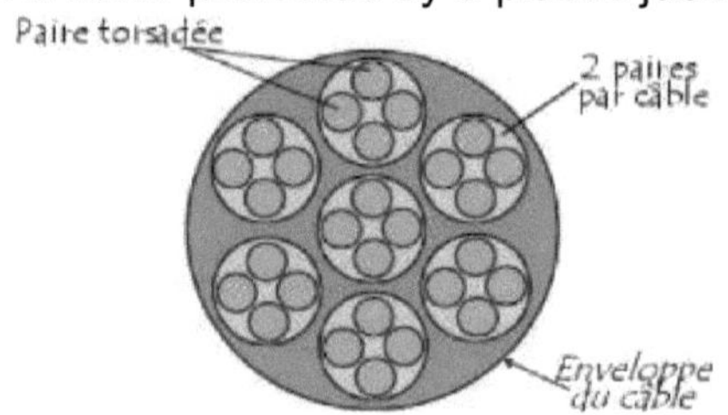

used on the telephone network comprise 2 to 2,400 pairs and are not shielded.

Traditional telephone services require a bandwidth of 3.1 kHz (the bandwidth between 3oo Hz and 3400 Hz), but the cables linking telephone exchanges to users all have a higher bandwidth, of the order of several hundred kHz. It was on this cable access network that the new technologies were developed.

xDSL techniques.

At high frequencies, distance-related problems are the most restrictive (attenuation, crosstalk, phase distortion). At low frequencies, problems associated with impulse noise dominate without too much difficulty up to 1 MHz. Beyond that, their use becomes tricky and requires high-performance transmission systems.

The limitations of the analogue network

The maximum possible bit rate on the analogue network is 33,600 bit/s in upstream mode and 56,000 (theoretical) in downstream mode.

It is easy to see why a technology that goes beyond the 3.1 kHz bandwidth is needed. The use of an ISDN connection in fact already makes use of xDSL technology, since it covers a frequency spectrum of up to 80 kHz. As explained in section 2.3.1, the CAP modulation technique was abandoned in favour of the DMT technique, which was adopted for the ANSI T1.413-1995 standard.

DMT (Discrete Multi Tone) is a form of multicarrier modulation. In its application to ADSL, the frequency spectrum between 0 Hz and 1.104 MHz is divided into 256 distinct sub-channels spaced at 4.3125 kHz. The lower sub-channels are generally reserved for POTS, so sub-channels 1 to 6 (up to 25.875 kHz) are in principle unused and left for analogue telephony.

According to T1.413, only sub-channels 1 to 31 can be used for upstream flow.

The upstream and downstream rates are separated either by EC (Echo Cancelling), which allows the lower sub-channels (from 1 to 31) to be used for downstream and upstream, or by FDM (Frequency Division Multiplexing), which is the most widely used because of its simplicity and low cost, separating the upstream/downstream sub-channels by a passive filter.

Distribution of DMT channels on POTS with EC

Subchannels 1 to 6 are used for telephony, subchannels 7 to 31 for uplink, subchannel 32 is reserved and subchannels 33 to 256 are used for downlink. It should be noted that sub-channels 16 and 64 are used to carry a pilot signal and that channels 250 to 256 can only be used on short connection lines. Above 1 MHz, the interference is too great to allow a stable flow.

In this case, DMT uses echo cancellation on these sub-channels, resulting in a duplex stream on sub-channels 7 to 31. If DMT had applied FDM, only the higher sub-channels (33 to 256) would be used for downstream.

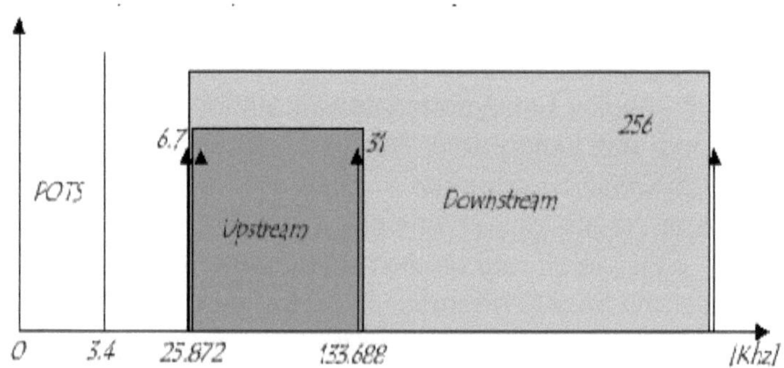

DMT channel allocation on ISDN with FDM

As we saw earlier, ISDN uses the lower bandwidth up to 80 KHz (for ISDN with 2B1Q - 2 Binary 1 Quaternary; coding of 2 binary elements in a quaternary modulation moment). To allow simultaneous use of ISDN and ADSL on the same telephone line, sub-channels 1 to 28 are freed up.

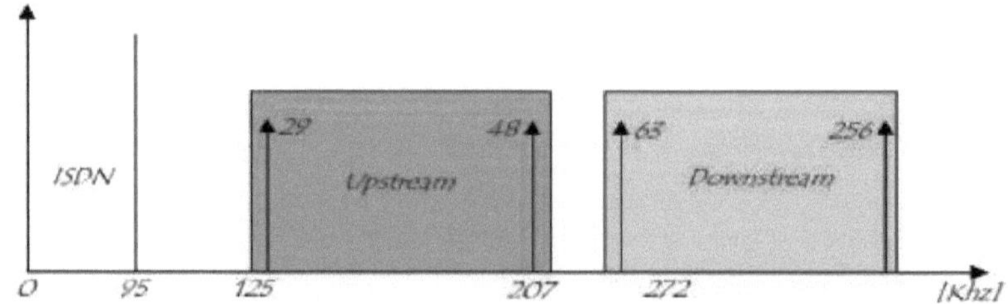

Lower channels are used for upstream throughput because user equipment has a lower transmission power than the equipment installed at the exchange, so by transmitting at lower frequencies, the signal will suffer less attenuation.

We use the upper channels for downstream throughput because the equipment located in the central office is strongly disturbed by high-frequency transmission equipment. It is therefore more efficient to transmit in the upper channels in order to benefit from a better signal-to-noise ratio.

ADSL equipment
The DSLAM

The DSLAM (Digital Subscriber Line Access Multiplexer) is a piece of equipment generally installed in telephone exchanges to multiplex ATM flows to the transport network.

This element not only houses ADSL cards, but can also accommodate different DSL services such as SDSL or HDSL by inserting the corresponding multiplexing cards. Each card supports several ADSL modems. The elements grouped together in the DSLAM are called ATU-C (ADSL Transceiver Unit, Central office end). In fact, all the services available on the network (Internet, LAN-MAN-WAN, teleshopping, MPEG video) arrive via broadband at a DSLAM station and are then redistributed to users.

Maintenance and configuration of the DSLAM and ADSL equipment is carried out remotely.

ADSL modems and routers

We saw in the previous chapter how the data is sent back to the user. But now the user has to decode the data, and this is the role of the modem, known as the ATU-R (ADSL Transceiver Unit, Remote terminal end).

There are currently three types of modem, depending on the user's needs:

- With 10/100 baseT interface, for PCs equipped with Ethernet card. ATMD 25 for PCs equipped with ATM cards or for redistributing ADSL over an ATM network.

- With USB interface, for PCs equipped with USB interface. If the user wants to redistribute ADSL on his computer network, he will prefer to use a router with ADSL interface.

Splitter and microfilter

In any case, the splitter is installed in the telephone exchange, downstream of the DSLAM and audio switch. Then, if the user has an ISDN connection, they will have to install a splitter at home upstream of their modem and ISDN NT.

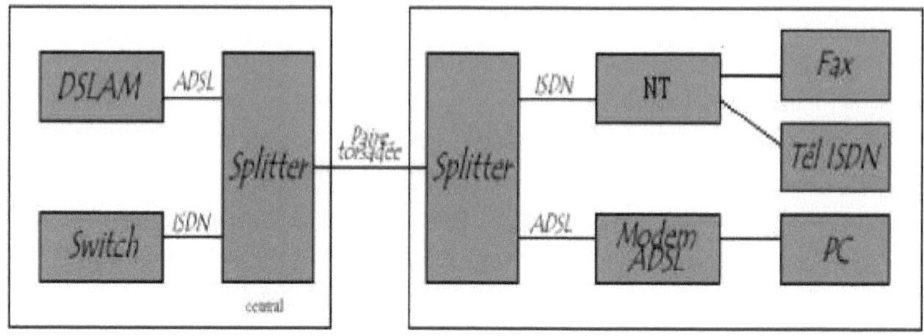

If the user has a traditional analogue connection, they do not need to install a splitter at home, but a microfilter before each telephone set.

Role of the splitter: the splitter is a switching filter that separates the bandwidth reserved for the telephone service from the bandwidth used for ADSL transmission. It provides sufficient decoupling to prevent signals transmitted on one of the frequency bands from interfering with the operation of the other. Installation of the splitter is compulsory for ADSL with an ISDN connection.

Role of the microfilter: the microfilter is a low-pass filter and is installed on the analogue connections. There is therefore no need to install a splitter.

The splitter and microfilter

Thanks to the DVB-T (Digital Video Broadcasting) digital terrestrial broadcasting standard, it is now possible to receive digital TV in MPEG format on a set-top box connected to a TV set.

For the moment, there is no set-top box on the market with an integrated ADSL modem. So you need an ADSL modem to which you can connect the MPEG DVB-T decoder, which is then linked to a TV set.

10 - Introduction to local loop unbundling

The **"local loop"** is the final part of the telephone line reaching the subscriber. To enable you to benefit from high-speed Internet access (ADSL), Internet Service Providers (ISPs) have to install equipment to connect to their servers in the incumbent operator's telephone exchanges, i.e. the **NRAs** (*subscriber connection nodes*) to which subscribers' telephone lines are routed. The aim of unbundling is to give ISPs access to the local loop (complete or otherwise). In the case of partial unbundling, the line is maintained by the incumbent operator and only the frequencies used to carry anything other than voice are leased (< 4 KHz). In the case of full unbundling, the ISP is responsible for line maintenance and passes on the price of the main subscription to the price of the ADSL subscription. However, full unbundling is rarely used by operators.

The incumbent operator must open the doors of its NRAs to other Internet Service Providers, so that they can install their own equipment in a special room. By law, France Telecom, the incumbent operator in France, has three months in which to make an NRA available to an ISP requesting it. During these three months, the incumbent operator must create two rooms in the NRA:

- a room dedicated to the dispatcher,
- and an "unbundling" or *co-location* room.

The equipment installed by ISPs in the unbundling room is called a **DSLam** (*Digital Suscriber Line Access Multiplexer*). DSLams are connected directly to the ISP's servers via fibre-optic links. These DSLAMs can be used to multiplex several types of data (in particular voice over IP, television and the Internet).

Let's summarise the path taken by your data during an unbundled ADSL connection:

- A subscriber's telephone socket is connected to an incumbent operator's distribution frame (the connection point for the entire neighbourhood) located in an NRA ;
- This distribution frame is itself connected to a mirror head, which is the point of division between the distribution frame room and the unbundling room, where the ISP takes over;
- The mirror heads are connected to the DSLAMs of the various ISPs in the unbundling room.
- These DSLAMs are in turn connected to the ISPs' servers via dedicated links (usually fibre optic).

CHAPTER 7

COMPUTER NETWORKS
WIRELESS

A wireless *network* is, as its name suggests, a network in which at least two terminals can communicate without a wired link. Thanks to wireless networks, a user can stay connected while moving around a more or less large geographical area, which is why we sometimes hear the term "mobility" used.

Wireless networks are based on a link using radio waves (radio and infrared) instead of the usual cables. There are a number of technologies, which differ in terms of the transmission frequency used, as well as the speed and range of transmissions.

Wireless networks make it very easy to link up equipment located anywhere from ten metres to a few kilometres apart. What's more, the installation of such networks does not require any major alterations to existing infrastructures, as is the case with wired networks (digging trenches to run the cables, equipping buildings with cabling, trunking and connectors), which has led to the rapid development of this type of technology.

On the other hand, there is the problem of regulation of radio transmissions. Radio transmissions are used for a large number of applications (military, scientific, amateur, etc.), but they are sensitive to interference, which is why regulations are needed in each country to define the frequency ranges and powers at which it is possible to transmit for each category of use.

What's more, radio waves are difficult to confine to a small geographical area, so it's easy for a hacker to eavesdrop on the network if the information is transmitted unencrypted (which is the default situation). It is therefore necessary to put in place the necessary measures to ensure the confidentiality of data circulating on wireless networks.

Wireless network categories

There are usually several categories of wireless networks, depending on the geographical area offering connectivity (known as the *coverage area*):

Wireless personal area networks (WPAN)

Wireless Personal Area Networks (WPANs) are wireless networks with a short range of a few tens of metres. This type of network is generally used to link peripherals (printers, mobile phones, domestic appliances, etc.) or a personal digital assistant (PDA) to a computer without a wired link, or to enable a wireless link between two machines that are very close together. There are several technologies used for WPANs:

The main *WPAN* technology is **Bluetooth**, launched by Ericsson in 1994, with a theoretical data rate of 1 Mbps and a maximum range of around thirty metres.

Bluetooth, also known as *IEEE 802.15.1*, has the advantage of using very little energy, making it particularly suitable for use in small devices.

HomeRF (for *Home Radio Frequency*), launched in 1998 by the HomeRF Working Group (including manufacturers Compaq, HP, Intel, Siemens, Motorola and Microsoft), offers a theoretical data rate of 10 Mbps with a range of around 50 to 100 metres without an amplifier. The HomeRF standard, supported in particular by Intel, was abandoned in January 2003, mainly because processor founders are now focusing on on-board Wi-Fi technologies (via *Centrino* technology, in which a microprocessor and Wi-Fi adapter are embedded in the same component).

ZigBee technology (also known as *IEEE 802.15.4*) provides wireless links at very low cost and with very low energy consumption, making it particularly suitable for direct integration into small electronic devices (household appliances, hi-fi, toys, etc.).

Lastly, **infrared** links can be used to create wireless links a few metres long, with data rates that can be as high as a few megabits per second. This technology is widely used for home automation (remote controls), but suffers from disruption caused by light interference. The irDA *(infrared data association),* formed in 1995, has over 150 members.

Wireless local area networks (WLAN)

The *Wireless Local Area Network* (**WLAN**) is a network that covers the equivalent of a company LAN, i.e. a range of around 100 metres. It enables terminals within the coverage area to be linked together. There are several competing technologies:

<u>Wifi</u> (or <u>IEEE 802.11</u>), supported by the <u>WECA</u> (Wireless Ethernet Compatibility Alliance) offers speeds of up to 54Mbps over a distance of several hundred metres.

hiperLAN2 (*HIgh Performance Radio LAN 2.0*), a European standard developed by ETSI (*European Telecommunications Standards Institute*). HiperLAN 2 delivers a theoretical data rate of 54 Mbps over an area of around 100 metres in the frequency range between 5,150 and 5,300 MHz.

HiperLAN2

Wireless metropolitan area networks (WMAN)

The *Wireless Metropolitan Area Network* (**WMAN**) is known as a **Radio Local Loop** (*RLL*). WMANs are based on the *IEEE 802.16* standard. The radio local loop offers a useful data rate of 1 to 10 Mbit/s for a range of 4 to 10 kilometres, which is why this technology is mainly used by telecoms operators.

Wireless Wide Area Networks (WWAN)

The *Wireless Wide Area Network* (**WWAN**) is also known as the *mobile cellular network*. These are the most widespread wireless networks, since all mobile phones are connected to a wireless wide area network. The main technologies are as follows:

- **GSM** (*Global System for Mobile Communication*)
- **GPRS** (*General Packet Radio Service*)
- **UMTS** (*Universal Mobile Telecommunication System*) Radio wave propagation

In order to set up a wireless network architecture, and in particular to position the access terminals (*access points*) in such a way as to obtain optimum range, it is necessary to have a minimum knowledge of the propagation of radio waves. Radio waves (*RF* stands for *Radio Frequency*) propagate in a straight line in several directions. The propagation speed of waves in a vacuum is 3.10^8 m/s.

In any other environment, the signal is attenuated by

. Reflection
- Refraction

- Diffraction
- Absorption

Absorption of radio waves

When a radio wave encounters an obstacle, some of its energy is absorbed and transformed into energy, some continues to propagate at an attenuated level and some may be reflected.

The reduction in the power of a signal during transmission is called **attenuation**. Attenuation is measured in bels (symbol B) and is equal to the logarithm to base 10 of the power at the output of the transmission medium, divided by the power at the input. We generally prefer to use the *decibel* (whose symbol is *dB*) corresponding to one tenth of the value in Bels. One Bel represents 10 decibels, so the formula becomes: R (dB) = (10) * log (P2/P1)

When R is positive we talk about *amplification*, when it is negative we talk about *attenuation*. In the case of wireless transmissions, this is more specifically attenuation.

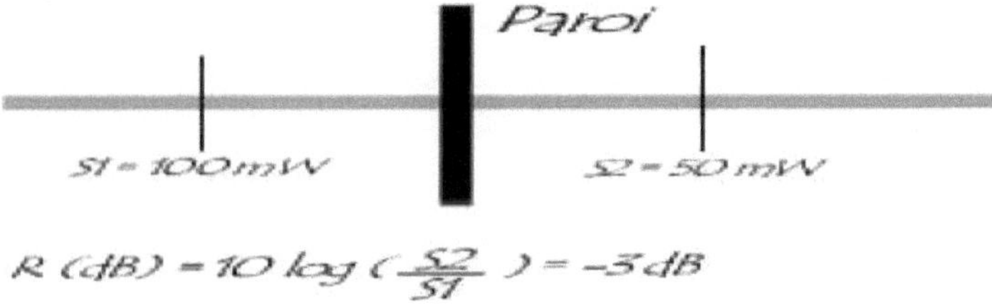

Attenuation increases with increasing frequency or distance. What's more, when you collide with an obstacle, the amount of attenuation depends very much on the material of which the obstacle is made. Metallic obstacles generally cause a strong reflection, while water absorbs the signal.

Reflection of radio waves

When a radio wave encounters an obstacle, all or part of the wave is reflected, with a loss of power. The reflection is such that the angle of incidence is equal to the angle of reflection.

O∧⅛⅛ ⅛X7⅛7⅛i⅞⅛¹ J⅝⅞⅞⅛⅛³

By definition, a radio wave can propagate in several directions. By successive reflections, a source signal can reach a station or access point by taking multiple *paths* (known as *multipath*).

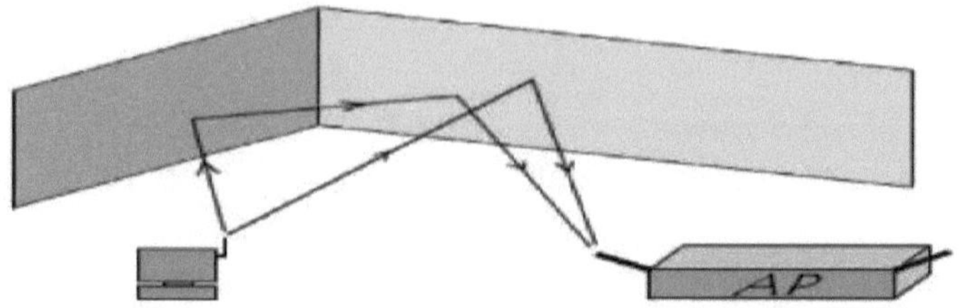

The difference in propagation times (known as *propagation delay*) between two signals that have taken different paths can cause interference at the receiver because the data received overlaps.

This interference becomes increasingly significant as transmission speed increases, because the time intervals between data are shorter and shorter. Multiple propagation paths therefore limit transmission speed in wireless networks.

To overcome this problem, Wi-Fi cards and access points incorporate two antennas per transmitter. Thanks to the action of the *AGC* (*Aquisition Gain Controller*), which immediately switches from one antenna to the other depending on the signal strength, the access point is able to distinguish between two signals coming from the same station. The signals received by these two antennas are said to be *decorrelated* (independent) if they are separated by Lambda/2 (6.25 cm at 2.4GHz).

Properties of media

The attenuation of signal power is largely due to the properties of the medium through which the wave travels. Here is a table showing the attenuation levels for different materials:

Materials	Weakening	Examples
Air	No	Open space, courtyard
Wood	Low	Door, floor, partition
Plastic	Low	Partition
Glass	Low	Non-tinted windows
Tinted glass	Medium	Tinted windows
Water	Medium	Aquarium, fountain
Living beings	Medium	Crowds, animals, humans, vegetation
Bricks	Medium	Walls
Plaster	Medium	Partitions
Ceramics	High	Tiling
Paper	High	Paper rolls
Concrete	High	Load-bearing walls, floors, pillars

Armoured glass	High	Bullet-proof glass
Metal	Very high	Reinforced concrete, mirrors, metal cabinet, lift shaft

There are different The equipment used for the installation of a Wifi wireless network :

- **Wireless** *adapters* or *network interface controllers* (*NICs*): these are 802.11 standard network cards that enable a machine to connect to a wireless network. WiFi adapters are available in many formats (PCI card, PCMCIA card, USB adapter, CompactFlash card, etc.).

Any equipment with such a card is referred to as a **station**.

- **Access points** (**AP** for *Access Point,* sometimes called *wireless terminals*) are used to provide access to the wired network (to which it is connected) to neighbouring stations equipped with WiFi cards.

The 802.11 standard defines two operating modes:

• The infrastructure mode in which wireless clients are connected to an access point. This is generally the default mode for 802.11b cards.

• Ad hoc mode in which clients are connected to each other without any access point.

Infrastructure mode

In **infrastructure mode**, each computer station (**STA**) connects to an access point via a wireless link. The set formed by the access point and the stations located in its coverage area is called a *basic service set* (**BSS**) and constitutes a cell. Each *BSS* is identified by a *BSSID*, a 6-byte (48-bit) identifier. In *infrastructure* mode, the *BSSID* corresponds to the MAC address of the access point.

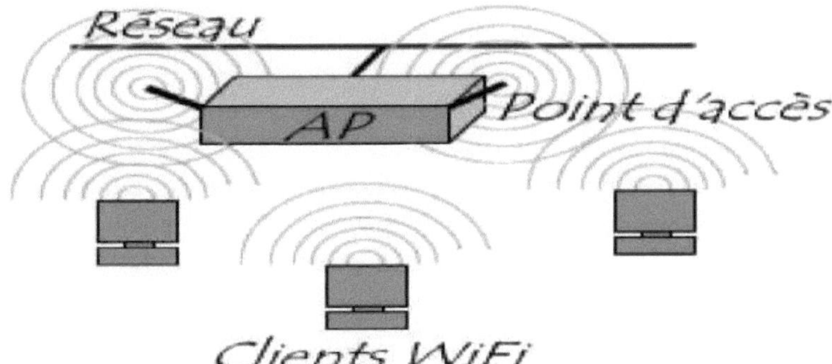

Several access points (or, more precisely, several *BSSs*) can be linked together by a link known as a *distribution system* (**DS** for *Distribution*

System) to form an *extended service set* (*ESS*). The distribution system (*DS*) can be a wired network, a cable between two access points or even a wireless network!

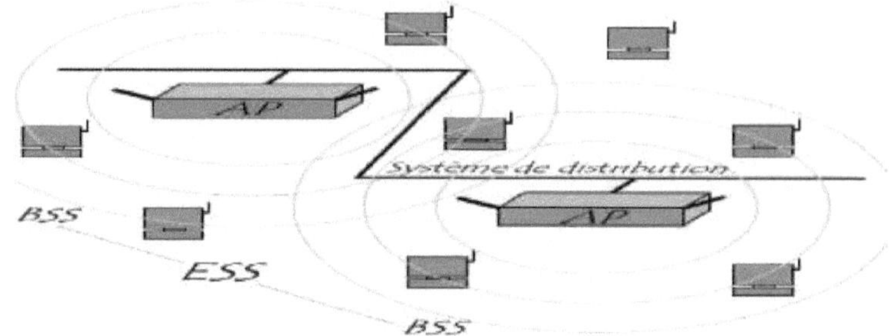

An *ESS* is identified by an **ESSID** (*Service Set Identifier*), i.e. a 32-character identifier (in ASCII format) used as a name for the network. The *ESSID*, often abbreviated to **SSID**, is the name of the network and represents a first level of security in that knowledge of the **SSID** is required for a station to connect to the WAN.

When a mobile user moves from one *BSS* to another as they move around the *ESS*, the wireless network adapter on their machine is able to change access points depending on the quality of reception of the signals from the different access points. The access points communicate with each other via the distribution system in order to exchange information about the stations and, if necessary, transmit data from the mobile stations. This feature, which allows stations to "move seamlessly" from one access point to another, is known as **roaming**.

Communication with the access point

When a station enters a cell, it broadcasts a *probe* request on each channel containing the *ESSID* for which it is configured and the data rates supported by its wireless adapter. If no *ESSID* is configured, the station listens to the network looking for an *SSID*.

Each access point regularly broadcasts (at a rate of one transmission every 0.1 seconds or so) a **beacon frame** giving information about its *BSSID*, its characteristics and possibly its *ESSID*. The *ESSID* is automatically broadcast by default, but it is possible (and recommended) to disable this option.

Each time a poll request is received, the access point checks the *ESSID* and the rate request in the *beacon frame*. If the *ESSID* matches that of the access point, the latter sends a response containing information about its load and synchronisation data. The station receiving the response can thus see the quality of the signal emitted by the access point in order to judge how far away it is. Generally speaking, the closer an access point is, the better the throughput.

A station within range of several access points (obviously with the same *SSID*) will be able to **choose** the access point offering the best compromise between throughput and load.

Ad hoc mode

In **ad hoc mode**, wireless client machines connect to each other to form a *peer-to-peer* network, i.e. a network in which each machine acts simultaneously as a client and an access point.

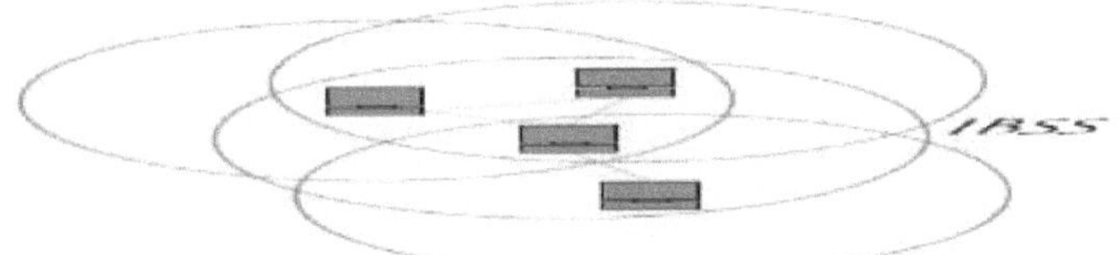

The set formed by the different stations is called an **independent** *basic* **service set** (*IBSS*).

An *IBSS* is a wireless network made up of at least two stations and does not use an access point. The *IBSS* is therefore an ephemeral network enabling people in the same room to exchange data. It is identified by an *SSID*, as is an *ESS* in infrastructure mode.

In an ad hoc network, the range of the *independent BSS* is determined by the range of each station. This means that if two of the network stations are out of range of each other, they will not be able to communicate, even if they "see" other stations. Unlike infrastructure mode, *ad hoc* mode does not offer a *distribution system* capable of transmitting frames from one station to another. An *IBSS* is therefore by definition a restricted wireless network.

CONCLUSION

This manual is the result of a lot of hard work and scientific gymnastics, and it is available to any researcher who is given the opportunity to do better.

At least some of the important concepts of computer networks have been described so that all readers have a basic idea of what they are.

Its use will provide knowledge of computer networks: structure, composition, data transmission, equipment, etc.

Implementation, on the other hand, will depend on the level of its culture.

Computing is a vast field, and everyone is being given the opportunity to continue with it, in order to ease the difficulties encountered, especially in documentation.

For any shortcomings noted here, we ask you not to hold it against us, for man is weak: "He who loves science, loves correction".

All comments are welcome.

"The Author

BIBLIOGRAPHY

Publications

1- Claude SERVIRE, Réseaux et Télécoms, Dunod, Paris, 2009

2- Guy PUJOLLE, Les réseaux, Edition Eyrolles, Paris, 2008

3- Jean François PILLOU, Commentçamarche, 2009

4- LESCOP YVES, Architecture des réseaux locaux, University of Toulouse, 2002, Unpublished

5- R. PEZO N. BIYO, Initiation à la théorie et à la pratique du réseau informatique, CRIGED, Kinshasa 2012 ;

6- Romain Jalloul, Nadia El Akremi, Mohamed Ben Rhouma, Operating System and Computer Networks, Centre National Pédagogique, Tunisian (-)

Other sources

1- Understanding the computer, What is the internet?

2- Microbiology course, 4th Humanities

3- Mukedi Diesta-Mputu Delphin, Conception d'un système informatique de gestion des impôts et taxes à payer d'une entreprise, Licence thesis, ISIPA, Kinshasa, 1994.

4- Mukedi Diesta-Mputu Delphin, Notes de Cours de Système d'exploitation Comparé, au deuxième Cycle Informatique (Réseau et Conception de Système d'Information) [unpublished].

http://www.person.clucb_internet.fr

www.wikipedia.org

www. Mémoire online

www.yumens.fr

I want morebooks!

Buy your books fast and straightforward online - at one of world's fastest growing online book stores! Environmentally sound due to Print-on-Demand technologies.

Buy your books online at
www.morebooks.shop

Kaufen Sie Ihre Bücher schnell und unkompliziert online – auf einer der am schnellsten wachsenden Buchhandelsplattformen weltweit! Dank Print-On-Demand umwelt- und ressourcenschonend produziert.

Bücher schneller online kaufen
www.morebooks.shop

info@omniscriptum.com
www.omniscriptum.com

Printed by Books on Demand GmbH, Norderstedt / Germany